NORDIC KNITS
WITH BIRGER BERGE

Traditional Patterns, Exciting New Looks

Birger Berge

TRAFALGAR SQUARE
North Pomfret, Vermont

First published in the United States of America
in 2020 by
Trafalgar Square Books
North Pomfret, Vermont 05053

Originally published in Norwegian as *Moderne Tradisjonsstrikk*.

ISBN: 978-1-64601-034-9
Library of Congress Control Number: 2020943910

Photographer: Tove Lise Mossestad
Cover Design: RM Didier
Interior Layout: Bente C. Bergan
Translation: Carol Huebscher Rhoades

Printed in China
10 9 8 7 6 5 4 3 2 1

TABLE OF CONTENTS

PREFACE

When I launched my Instagram account in 2016, I never thought it would become such a large and important part of my life. When I had to decide on a name for my account, my first thought was something knitting-related, but I decided against that; I was afraid it would be too pretentious. Besides, I wasn't sure whether my account would end up dedicated solely to knitting, and I definitely didn't expect it would become as big as it has.

The solution was to use my own name. My parents had astutely given me a short and alliterative name, easy to remember and certainly good enough for Instagram. And my parents also probably deserve the biggest thanks for the existence of this book. I was always different from my brothers, and from most of the other boys I knew growing up, and they accepted that fact early on. It was never a problem for them that I liked dolls, or that I liked to wear skirts, or that one of the finest things I owned was a little apron with small hearts on it.

When I was old enough for it, I was allowed to learn to sew and knit, activities I loved the moment I tried them. At school, this became a problem; I was outed and was often bullied. It wasn't exactly "cool" to be able to pull up the bobbin thread on the sewing machine, and I'd probably have had an easier time of it if I'd been good at soccer and sports instead. But I continued on my own path, and the love and acceptance of my parents and my brothers made me confident enough to be comfortable being myself. For example, the most popular elective in my final year of junior high school was moped repair, but I chose to crochet a tablecloth instead. Looking back, I'm very proud that I made that

choice, because I can remember vividly how nervous I was about it and how much flak I got for it.

So my interest in exploring creativity and handcrafting techniques was well-established at an early age. It became even more important to me going forward, during and after university—much of what I studied and my work in later jobs has been theoretical and data-based. It isn't just about creating lovely, warm, practical clothing; there's a tactile beauty to knitting, and being able to create something with my own two hands. The tradition of handcrafting matters to me in more than one way. Not only is it important to me to know that I'm part of Norway's knitting history and culture, it's also a deeply personal presence in my life. I've always loved to create, whether on paper, with fabric, or with yarn.

Although my Instagram account is mostly knitting aesthetics and projects, I hope that many knitters have gotten to know me better through it. But there's something special about the process of creating a book, knowing people will buy it and hold it in their hands. I've been working on it for a long time, and the patterns are, in a way, a part of me.

I can only hope that as you look through the book, you'll like the patterns and be inspired to knit some of them. The best thing about designing patterns is the opportunity to encourage others to knit them and bring them to life in their own way.

Bergen, April 2019
Birger Berge

TIPS AND ADVICE

CASTING ON AND BINDING OFF

There are many methods for casting on and binding off. Most often you can use the method you prefer, with a few exceptions. For the half-star slippers, you'll need to use a loop cast-on or "Judy's Magic Cast-on." You can find instructional videos for these techniques on YouTube, as well as other techniques for casting on invisibly (meaning the cast-on row looks like any other knit row). These methods are most commonly used for toe-up socks.

Some of the patterns recommend that you sew a neat edge in finishing. For these, I prefer Kitchener stitch, which yields the same results as the loop cast-on. The bind-off looks like a knitted edge instead of looking as if the yarn had been drawn through the stitches at the end and tightened.

HEELS AND THUMBS

For many of the patterns, you will knit in a smooth, contrast-color scrap yarn, which you will later remove before knitting the thumb or heel. When the scrap yarn is removed, and you begin to knit in the round, you might find that there are little holes at the sides of the thumb or heel. You can avoid the holes by casting on or picking up and knitting an extra stitch at each side which you can decrease on the next round so you will have the correct stitch count.

GAUGE

Gauge is very important. Even if a pattern lists a specific needle size, that doesn't mean using that needle size guarantees your knitting will match the pattern's gauge. Before you begin knitting, you should always knit a gauge swatch—or be prepared to rip out and start over with a needle in a different size. If the yarn and needle size are the same for a larger project as for a smaller one like a matching hat, consider knitting the hat as your "swatch," so you can test the yarn and needles and see how they feel to you.

SHAPING THE BACK AND FRONT NECK

On pullovers and cardigans, the instructions often suggest placing the stitches for the front neck on a holder and continuing to work the back. That's because these garments will fit better if the back neck is higher. Many designers recommend using short rows to achieve the extra height, but you can also knit back backwards, from right to left and from left to right. Make sure to "twist" the stitches to sit correctly when you work this way so you don't end up with twisted knit stitches.

EVEN KNITTING

For even results in stranded colorwork knitting, it's important to hold the yarns in the same positions relative to each other throughout. If you swap the positions of the main and contrast color yarns on your fingers, the balance between the colors will also change, and your pattern will be distorted.

REINFORCED HEELS AND TOES

All of my sock patterns are worked in two-color stranded knitting. This method makes the socks not only warmer but also stronger. To ensure that the gauge stays consistent throughout, and to strengthen the heels and toes at the same time, you can work the heels and toes with two strands of the same single color, working as for two-color knitting by alternating the strands. Heels and toes worked with doubled yarn will be much more durable.

WASHING

You should avoid washing wool garments more than absolutely necessary. It's usually sufficient to simply air out woolens. If you do need to wash the garment, in order to better preserve it, use the wool (gentle) program on your washing machine and wool-safe soap.

GARMENT EASE

The patterns in this book for larger garments such as pullovers and cardigans allow 1¼ in / 3 cm ease for a close-fitting garment. If you want a more loosely fitted garment, you can either knit a larger size or work at a looser gauge. A good starting point for determining the ideal size and fit for you is to measure a garment that fits you well and knit your new garment in a corresponding size.

ABBREVIATIONS AND TERMS

BO	bind off (= UK cast off)	MC	main (background) color	steek	A section of extra stitches added so you can knit in the round on a sweater body that will later be cut open—for the two fronts of a cardigan, or for the armholes from underarms to shoulders, or for the neck (for example, to form a placket). Usually steek stitches are worked in alternating pattern colors, or with one color for single-color rounds. Instructions for working steek stitches and for reinforcing and cutting a steek are given in individual patterns.
CC	contrast (or pattern) color	m	meter(s)		
ch	chain st	mm	millimeters		
cm	centimeters	p	purl		
CO	cast on	pm	place marker		
dpn	double-pointed needles	psso	pass slipped st over		
est	established = continue pattern as set	RLI	right-lifted increase: knit into right side of st below st on needle and then knit st on needle		
in	inch(es)				
k	knit				
k2tog	knit 2 together = 1 stitch decreased; right-leaning decrease	RS	right side		
		rem	remain(s)(ing)		
		rep	repeat		
K-CO	knitted cast-on: knit into previous st on left needle, *place new loop knitwise on left needle and knit into it*; rep from *to * for desired number of sts.	rnd(s)	round(s)		
		sc	single crochet (= British double crochet)		
		sl m	slip marker		
		ssk	[slip 1 knitwise] 2 times, knit the 2 sts together through back loops (= 1 stitch decreased; left-leaning decrease		
LLI	Left-lifted increase: knit st on left needle, leaving it on needle, knit into left side of 2nd st below st on needle				
		st(s)	stitch(es)		
		tbl	through back loop(s)		
M1	make 1 = increase 1 stitch by picking up the strand between two stitches with the left needle tip, from front to back, and knit directly into back loop	tog	together		
		WS	wrong side		
		yd	yards		
		yo	yarnover		
		–	repeat the sequence between the asterisks		

FLATEN PULLOVER

The Flaten Pullover and Flaten Cardigan are named for my relatives on my mother's side, and particularly for my maternal grandfather Olav Flaten, who was a kind, good, and vigorous man. Once I knitted and felted a pair of slippers for him with the Jølster municipality's coat of arms embroidered on them; he liked them so much that he always set them right next to his favorite chair.

||||||||||||||||||||||||||||||||||||||||||||||||||||||||||||||||||||||

SKILL LEVEL
Experienced

SIZES
XS (S, M, L, XL, XXL)

FINISHED MEASUREMENTS
Chest: approx. 35½ (39½, 43¼, 47¼, 51¼, 55¼) in / 90 (100, 110, 120, 130, 140) cm
Total Length: approx. 23¾ (24½, 25½, 26¾, 27½, 28¼) in / 60 (62, 65, 68, 70, 72) cm
Sleeve Length: approx. 19¾ (19¾, 20, 20, 20½, 20½) in / 50 (50, 51, 51, 52, 52) cm

MATERIALS
Yarn:
CYCA #1 (fingering) Trollkar Supermjuk (Supersoft) (100% pure new wool, 383 yd/350 m / 100 g)

Yarn Colors and Amounts:
Golden Brown 292: 300 (350, 400, 400, 500, 500) g
Natural White 201: 300 (350, 350, 400, 450, 500) g

Needles:
U. S. sizes 1.5 and 2.5 / 2.5 and 3 mm: circulars and sets of 5 dpn.
NOTE: If you knit stranded colorwork more firmly than single-color knitting, you should go up a needle size.

GAUGE
26 sts in stockinette on larger needles = 4 in / 10 cm.
Adjust needle size to obtain correct gauge if necessary.

BODY
With Golden Brown and smaller circular, CO 230 (258, 282, 306, 334, 358) sts. Join, being careful not to twist cast-on row; pm for beginning of rnd). Work around in k1, p1 ribbing for 20 rnds.

Knit 1 rnd. Change to larger circular and Natural White. Knit 1 rnd, *at the same time* increasing 6 sts evenly spaced around = 236 (264, 288, 312, 340, 364) sts around, or 118 (132, 144, 156, 170, 182) sts each for front and back. Work 4 sts following Chart **B**, 113 (127, 139, 151, 165, 173) sts following Chart **A**, and 1 st following Chart **B** on front and back. In order to ensure that st 19 of Chart **A** will be at the center on both front and back, begin on st 36 (28, 22, 16, 9, 5) on Chart **A**. Continue as est until body measures 16½ (17, 17¼, 18¼, 18½, 19) in / 42 (43, 44, 46, 47, 48) cm or desired length to underarms. On the last rnd, BO or place on holders 11 (11, 13, 15, 17, 19) sts centered at each underarm = sts worked following Chart **B** + 3 (3, 4, 5, 6, 7) sts to either side. Set body aside while you knit the sleeves.

SLEEVES
With Golden Brown and smaller dpn, CO 56 (58, 60, 62, 64, 66) sts. Divide sts onto dpn and join; pm for beginning of rnd. Work around in k1, p1 ribbing for 20 rnds.

Change to larger dpn and knit 1 rnd. With Natural White, knit 1 rnd increasing 6 sts evenly spaced around = 62 (64, 66, 68, 70, 72) sts. The rnd begins at the center of each underarm with 4 sts following Chart **B**, then 57 (59, 61, 63, 65, 67) sts following Chart **A**, and 1 st from Chart **B**. Increase on each side of Chart **B** approx. every 4th rnd.

In order to ensure that st 19 of Chart **A** will be at center of sleeve, begin on st 26 (25, 24, 23, 22, 21) on Chart **A**. Continue as est following Charts **A** and **B**, increasing as described above until there are a total of 108 (110, 114, 118, 122, 130) sts and sleeve is 19¾ (19¾, 20, 20, 20½, 20½) in / 50 (50, 51, 51, 52, 52) cm long or desired length. BO or place on holders the center 11 (11, 13, 15, 17, 19) sts on underarm. Make sure you end on the same pattern row as for body when ending each sleeve. Set first sleeve aside while you knit second sleeve the same way.

JOINING BODY AND SLEEVES/ RAGLAN SHAPING

Now it's time to join the body and sleeves on larger circular = total of 408 (440, 464, 488, 516, 556) sts. The joins and sts where you will later decrease are indicated on Chart **B**. In order to ensure that the sts on Chart **B** are divided equally across the pieces (front, back, and sleeves), work the last 2 sts on the front and back and sleeves following Chart **B**, then CO 1 new st between the pieces, knitted as for st 3 on Chart **B**, before working the next 2 sts of front, back, and sleeves following Chart **B**, for a total of 5 sts following Chart **B** at each "join." The rest of the work is knitted following Chart **A** as before. Chart **A** will not fit evenly around—the pattern is broken after Chart **B**. Work 4 (8, 8, 8, 10, 10) rnds without decreasing, as for the joining rnd. Next, begin raglan shaping.

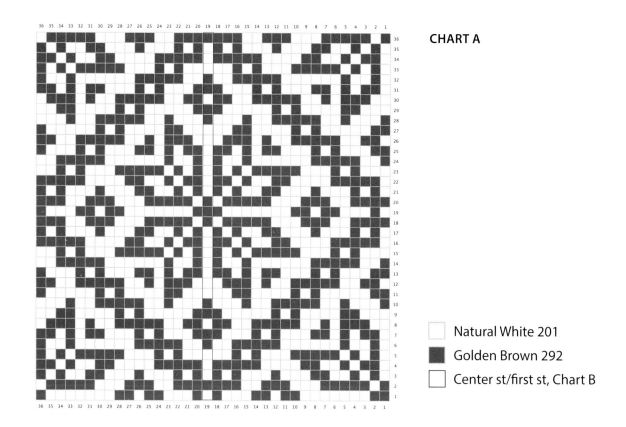

CHART A

☐ Natural White 201

■ Golden Brown 292

☐ Center st/first st, Chart B

Raglan Shaping: Always decrease with Natural White as follows: Knit until 2 sts before pattern worked following Chart **B**. K2tog with Natural White, k5 of Chart **B**. Decrease on the other side of Chart **B** with sl 1, k1 with Natural White, psso. You will decrease at different rates on the body and sleeves. On the body, decrease on every other rnd 16 times and on every rnd 19 (21, 23, 25, 27, 30) times. On the sleeves, decrease on every 4th rnd 4 times, on every other rnd 8 times, and then on every rnd 19 (21, 23, 25, 27, 30) times.

After all decreases, 144 (160, 168, 176, 188, 204) sts rem. Shape back neck, working back and forth. At front, place the center 23 (25, 27, 29, 31, 35) sts on a holder. While you knit back and forth in pattern following Chart **A** or **B**, place 8,6,4,2 (8,6,4,2,2; 8,6,4,2,2,2; 8,6,4,4,2,2,2; 8,6,4,4,2,2,2,2; 8,6,4,4,2,2,2,2,2) sts on a holder on each side of front neck. *At the same time*, continue shaping raglan on each side of the sts following Chart **B** as before. The total st count rem for neckband is 112 (120, 120, 120, 124, 132). Change to smaller circular and work 20 rnds in k1, p1 ribbing. BO loosely in ribbing. Fold neckband in half and sew down edge to WS.

Seam underarms.
Weave in all ends neatly on WS.

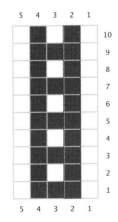

CHART B

FLATEN CARDIGAN

SKILL LEVEL
Experienced

SIZES
XS (S, M, L, XL, XXL)

FINISHED MEASUREMENTS
Chest: approx. 35½ (39½, 43¼, 47¼, 51¼, 55¼) in / 90 (100, 110, 120, 130, 140) cm
Total Length: approx. 23¾ (24½, 25½, 26¾, 27½, 28¼) in / 60 (62, 65, 68, 70, 72) cm
Sleeve Length: approx. 19¾ (19¾, 20, 20, 20½, 20½) in / 50 (50, 51, 51, 52, 52) cm

MATERIALS
Yarn:
CYCA #1 (fingering) Trollkar Supermjuk (Supersoft) (100% pure new wool, 383 yd/350 m / 100 g)

Yarn Colors and Amounts:
Charcoal Gray 209: 300 (350, 400, 400, 500, 500) g
Light Gray 202: 300 (350, 350, 400, 450, 500) g

Needles:
U. S. sizes 1.5 and 2.5 / 2.5 and 3 mm: circulars and sets of 5 dpn.
NOTE: If you knit stranded colorwork more firmly than single-color knitting, you should go up a needle size.

Notions:
10 buttons

GAUGE
26 sts in stockinette on larger needles = 4 in / 10 cm.
Adjust needle size to obtain correct gauge if necessary.

BODY

With Charcoal Gray and smaller circular, CO 246 (274, 298, 322, 350, 374) sts. Work back and forth in k1, p1 ribbing for 20 rnds. **NOTE:** On the 11th row of ribbing, make a buttonhole on the right side, 3 sts inside the edge: BO 2 sts. On Row 12, CO 2 sts over the gap. Continue in ribbing to last row. Place the first and last 8 sts on each side on holders for the front bands = 230 (258, 282, 306, 334, 358) sts rem for body. CO 5 sts at center front for steek (steek sts are not included in st counts). Join to work in the round.

Knit 1 rnd. Change to larger circular and Light Gray. Knit 1 rnd, increasing 7 sts evenly spaced around = 237 (265, 289, 313, 341, 365) sts, with 119 (133, 145, 157, 171, 183) sts for the back and 59 (66, 72, 78, 85, 91) sts for each front. The rnd begins at the front steek. On the first front piece, knit the 57 (64, 70, 76, 83, 89) sts from st 1 to the right on Chart **A**, then 2 sts from Chart **B**. On the back, work the next 3 sts following Chart **B** (a total of 5 sts from Chart **B** divided over the front and back), then 113 (127, 139, 151, 165, 177) sts following Chart **A** on the back, and 3 sts from Chart **B**. In order to ensure that st 19 on Chart **A** is centered on the back, begin on st 36 (28, 22, 16, 9, 5) of Chart **A**. On the opposite front, begin with 2 sts of Chart **B**, then 57 (64, 70, 76, 83, 89) sts following Chart **A**, but reversed to correspond so that st 1 of Chart **A** is at center front inside the steek.

Work following Charts **A** and **B** until body measures 16½ (17, 17¼, 18¼, 18½, 19) in / 42 (43, 44, 46, 47, 48) cm or desired length to underarms. On the last rnd, BO or place on holders 11 (11, 13, 15, 17, 19) sts centered at each underarm. Set body aside while you knit the sleeves.

SLEEVES

With Charcoal Gray and smaller dpn, CO 56 (58, 60, 62, 64, 66) sts. Divide sts onto dpn and join; pm for beginning of rnd. Work around in k1, p1 ribbing for 20 rnds.

Change to larger dpn and knit 1 rnd. Knit 1 rnd in Light Gray and, *at the same time*, increase 6 sts evenly spaced around = 62 (64, 66, 68, 70, 72) sts. The rnd begins at the center of each underarm with 4 sts following Chart **B**, then 57 (59, 61, 63, 65, 67) sts following Chart **A**, and 1 st from Chart **B**. Increase on each side of Chart **B** approx. every 4th rnd. In order to ensure that st 19 of Chart **A** will be at center of sleeve, begin on st 26 (25, 24, 23, 22, 21) of Chart **A**. Continue as est following Charts **A** and **B**, increasing as noted above, working new sts into Chart **A** pattern, until there are a total of 108 (110, 114, 118, 122, 130) sts and sleeve is 19¾ (19¾, 20,

20, 20½, 20½) in / 50 (50, 51, 51, 52, 52) cm long or desired length. BO or place on holder the center 11 (11, 13, 15, 17, 19) sts on underarm.

Make sure you end on the same pattern row as for body when ending each sleeve. Set first sleeve aside while you knit second sleeve the same way.

JOINING/RAGLAN SHAPING

Now it's time to join the body and sleeves on larger circular = total of 408 (440, 464, 488, 516, 556) sts. The joins and sts where you will later decrease are indicated on Chart **B**. In order to ensure that the sts on Chart **B** are divided equally across the pieces (front, back, and sleeves), work the last 2 sts on the front and back and sleeves following Chart **B**, then CO 1 new st between the pieces, knitted as the 3rd st on Chart **B**, and then work the next 2 sts of front, back, and sleeves following Chart **B**, for a total of 5

CHART A

CHART B

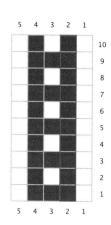

☐ Light Gray 202

■ Charcoal Gray 209

☐ Center st/first st, Chart B

sts following Chart B at each "join." The rest of the sts are worked following Chart **A** as before the joining. Chart **A** will not fit evenly around—the pattern is broken after Chart **B**.

Raglan Shaping: Always decrease with Light Gray as follows: Knit until 2 sts before pattern of Chart **B**. K2tog with Light Gray, k5 of Chart **B**. Decrease on the other side of the front band with sl 1, k1 with Light Gray, psso. You will decrease at different rates on the body and sleeves. On the body, decrease on every other rnd 16 times and on every rnd 19 (21, 23, 25, 27, 30) times. On the sleeves, decrease on every 4th rnd 4 times, on every other rnd 8 times, and then on every rnd 19 (21, 23, 25, 27, 30) times.

After all decreases, 144 (160, 168, 176, 188, 204) sts rem. Shape back neck, working back and forth. At each front, place the outer 11 (12, 14, 15, 16, 17) sts of neck on a holder; BO steek sts. While you knit back and forth in pattern from Charts **A** and **B**, place 8,6,4,2 (8,6,4,2,2; 8,6,4,2,2,2; 8,6,4,4,2,2,2; 8,6,4,4,2,2,2,2; 8,6,4,4,2,2,2,2,2) sts on a holder on each side of front neck. *At the same time*, continue shaping raglan on each side of the sts following Chart **B** as before. The total st count rem for neckband is 112 (120, 120, 120, 124, 132) sts.

FINISHING/FRONT BANDS

Reinforce the steek with crochet or machine stitching (you can find guides for each method on YouTube). Carefully cut steek open up center st. Place held sts of one band on a smaller needle and CO 8 new sts for a facing, to be sewn down later to cover cut steek sts. Work the 8 sts of button band in k1, p1 ribbing as est and work facing sts in stockinette. On the right front band, make a buttonhole approx. every 3 in / 7.5 cm as before. When band reaches neck, BO the 8 facing sts and place rem ribbing sts onto same needle as rem body sts. Work the opposite front band the same way, omitting buttonholes. When all rem body and front band sts are on same circular, there are a total of 128 (136, 136, 136, 140,

148) sts. Knit 1 row in Light Gray and then work 20 rows in k1 p1 ribbing. BO loosely in ribbing. Sew front bands to front edges. Fold facing over cut edges and sew down smoothly on WS. Fold neckband in half and sew down edge to WS.

Seam underarms. Weave in all ends neatly on WS. Gently steam press cardigan under damp pressing cloth.

FEELING GOOD PULLOVER

For this pullover, I chose colors that reminded me of sunlight reflected in a fjord. Because I am from the sunniest fjord county—or, as it's sometimes called, the "county of well-being"— the name of this sweater had to be the Feeling Good Pullover.

||||||||||||||||||||||||||||||||||||||||||||||||||||||||||||||||||||||||||||||||||||||||||||||||||||||||||||||||||||||||||

SKILL LEVEL
Experienced

SIZES
XS (S, M, L, XL, XXL)

FINISHED MEASUREMENTS
Chest: approx. 35½ (39½, 43¼, 47¼, 51¼, 55¼) in / 90 (100, 110, 120, 130, 140) cm
Total Length: approx. 22½ (23¼, 24, 25¼, 26, 26¾) in / 57 (59, 61, 64, 66, 68) cm
Sleeve Length: approx. 19¾ (19¾, 20, 20, 20½, 20½) in / 50 (50, 51, 51, 52, 52) cm

MATERIALS
Yarn:
CYCA #3 (DK, light worsted) Hillesvåg Tinde pelsull-garn (100% Norwegian pelt sheep wool, 284 yd/260 m / 100 g)
CYCA #2 (sport, baby) Hillesvåg Sol Lamullgarn (100% Norwegian lamb's wool, 317 yd/290 m / 100 g)

Yarn Colors and Amounts:
Sol White 400: 100 (100, 100, 100, 100, 100) g
Tinde Light Turquoise 2130: 100 (100, 100, 100, 100, 100) g
Tinde Cognac 2103: 100 (100, 100, 100, 100, 100) g
Tinde Navy Blue 2133: 400 (400, 400, 400, 500, 500) g

Needles:
U. S. sizes 2.5 and 4 / 3 and 3.5 mm: circulars and sets of 5 dpn.
NOTE: If you knit stranded colorwork more firmly than single-color knitting, you should go up a needle size.

GAUGE
22 sts in stockinette on larger needles = 4 in / 10 cm.
Adjust needle size to obtain correct gauge if necessary.

CHART A

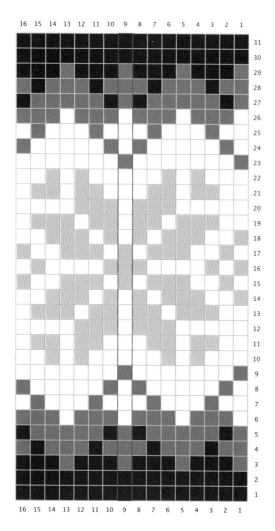

16 15 14 13 12 11 10 9 8 7 6 5 4 3 2 1

☐ White 400

■ Navy Blue 2133

■ Light Turquoise 2130

▨ Cognac 2103

☐ Center st

MEN

BODY

With Navy Blue and smaller circular, CO 178 (200, 222, 244, 266, 288) sts. Join, being careful not to twist cast-on row; pm for beginning of rnd. Work 15 rnds k1, p1 ribbing. Change to larger circular and knit 1 rnd, increasing 20 sts evenly spaced around = 198 (220, 242, 264, 286, 308) sts. Pm at each side with 99 (109, 121, 131, 143, 153) sts each for front and back. **NOTE:** Always purl the last st on front and back for side sts; all other sts are worked in stockinette. Continue until body measures 16½ (17, 17¼, 18¼, 18½, 19) in / 42 (43, 44, 46, 47, 48) cm. BO or place on holders the 7 (9, 11, 13, 13, 15) sts + the purl side st centered at each side for the underarms = 3 (4, 5, 6, 6, 7) sts on each side of side st. Set body aside while you knit the sleeves.

SLEEVES

With Navy Blue and smaller dpn, CO 44 (46, 48, 52, 56, 60) sts. Divide sts onto dpn and join. Work 15 rnds k1, p1 ribbing.

Change to larger dpn. Knit 1 rnd, increasing 6 sts evenly spaced around = 50 (52, 54, 58, 62, 66) sts. Always purl the st at center of underarm; all other sts are in stockinette. Approx. every 4th rnd, increase 1 st on each side of center st until st count is 92 (96, 98, 102, 106, 110) sts and sleeve is 19¾ (19¾, 20, 20, 20½, 20½) in / 50 (50, 51, 51, 52, 52) cm long. BO or place on holder the center 7 (9, 11, 13, 13, 15) sts on underarm = 3 (4, 5, 6, 6, 7) sts on each side of purl st + purl st. Set first sleeve aside while you knit second sleeve the same way.

JOINING/RAGLAN SHAPING

Now it's time to join the body and sleeves on larger circular. Begin with the front. At each intersection of body and sleeve, CO 1 purl st and pm for raglan shaping.

Knit 2 rnds. Now work in pattern following Chart **A**. In order to ensure that pattern is centered on front and back, begin on st 12 (8, 2, 14, 8, 4) on chart. Begin sleeves on st 15 (14, 14, 13, 11, 10) on chart. Knit 8 (8, 10, 10, 10, 10) rnds.

Raglan Shaping:
The decreases for raglan shaping occur before/after the purl st marked at each intersection of body and sleeve. The pattern will not come out evenly at the raglan lines. Decrease as well as possible in pattern color: k2tog before purl st, purl 1, sl 1, k1, psso after purl st. You will decrease at different rates on the body and sleeves. On the body, decrease on every other rnd 12 times and on every rnd 16 (18, 20, 22, 24, 26) times. On the sleeves, decrease on every 4th rnd 3 times, on every other rnd 6 times, and then on every rnd 16 (18, 20, 22, 24, 26) times.

After completing these decreases, BO or place on holder center front 19 (21, 23, 25, 27, 29) sts for front neck. Begin working back and forth and, on every row, at neck edge, set aside or BO 6,4,4,2 (6,4,4,2,2; 6,4,4,2,2,2; 6,4,4,4,2,2,2; 6,4,4,4,2,2,2,2) sts. *At the same time*, continue raglan decreases until 104 (106, 108, 112, 118) sts rem.

NECKBAND
Place held sts or pick up and knit sts around neck onto smaller circular; pm for beginning of rnd. Work around in k1, p1 ribbing for 3½ in / 9 cm. BO loosely in ribbing. Fold band in half and sew down edge on WS.

FINISHING
Seam underarm. Weave in all ends neatly on WS. Gentle steam press pullover under damp pressing cloth.

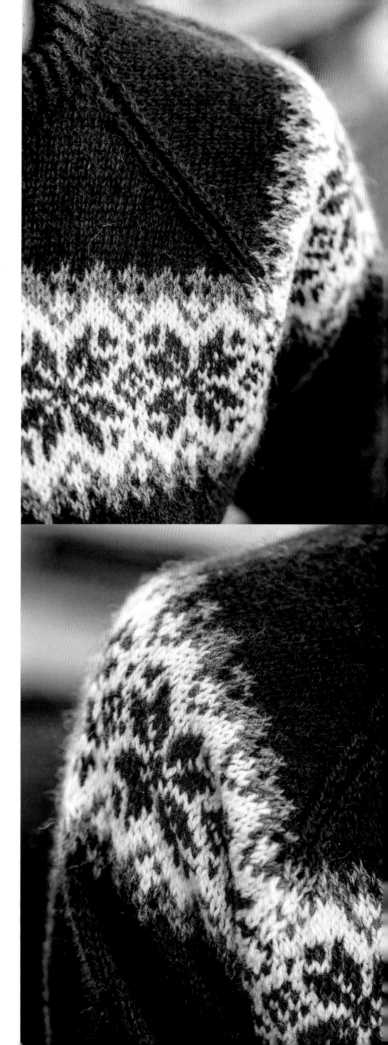

WOMEN

|||||||||||||||||||||||||||||||||||||||||||||||||||||||||||||||||||||||||||||||||||||||||||||||||||||||||||||||||||||||||||||||||||||||||||||

SKILL LEVEL
Experienced

SIZES
XS (S, M, L, XL, XXL, XXXL)

FINISHED MEASUREMENTS
Chest: approx. 33½ (37½, 41¼, 45¼, 49¼, 53¼, 57) in /
85 (95, 105, 115, 125, 135, 145) cm
Total Length: approx. 22½ (22¾, 23¼, 23¾, 24, 24½,
24¾) in / 57 (58, 59, 60, 61, 62, 63) cm
Sleeve Length: approx. 17¼ (17¾, 17¾, 17¾, 18¼,
18½, 18½) in / 44 (45, 45, 45, 46, 47, 47) cm

MATERIALS
Yarn:
CYCA #3 (DK, light worsted) Hillesvåg Tinde pelsull-
garn (100% Norwegian pelt sheep wool, 284 yd/260 m
/ 100 g)
CYCA #2 (sport, baby) Hillesvåg Sol Lamullgarn (100%
Norwegian lamb's wool, 317 yd/290 m / 100 g)

Yarn Colors and Amounts:
Sol Natural White 400: 100 (100, 100, 100, 100, 100,
100) g
Tinde Pink 2110: 100 (100, 100, 100, 100, 100, 100) g
Tinde Dark Brown 2116: 100 (100, 100, 100, 100, 100,
100) g
Tinde Burgundy-Purple 2132: 300 (300, 300, 400, 400,
400, 400) g

Needles:
U. S. sizes 2.5 and 4 / 3 and 3.5 mm: circulars and sets
of 5 dpn.
NOTE: If you knit stranded colorwork more firmly than
single-color knitting, you should go up a needle size.

GAUGE
22 sts in stockinette on larger needles = 4 in / 10 cm.
Adjust needle size to obtain correct gauge if necessary.

BODY

With Burgundy-Purple and smaller circular, CO 168 (190, 210, 230, 250, 276, 300) sts. Join, being careful not to twist cast-on row; pm for beginning of rnd. Work around in k1, p1 ribbing for 2 in / 5 cm. Change to larger circular and knit 1 rnd, increasing 20 sts evenly spaced around = 188 (210, 230, 250, 270, 296, 320) sts. Pm at each side = 94 (105, 115, 125, 135, 148, 160) sts each for back and front. Continue around in stockinette until body measures 15½ (15¾, 15¾, 16¼, 16¼, 16½, 16½) in / 39 (40, 40, 41, 41, 42, 42) cm. BO or place on holders the 6 (8, 10, 12, 14, 14, 18) sts centered on each underarm. Set body aside while you knit the sleeves.

SLEEVES

With Burgundy-Purple and smaller dpn, CO 42 (44, 46, 46, 50, 52, 54) sts. Divide sts onto dpn and join. Work around in k1, p1 ribbing for 2 in / 5 cm. Change to larger dpn. Knit 1 rnd, increasing 6 sts evenly spaced around = 48 (50, 52, 52, 56, 58, 60) sts. Always purl the st at center of underarm; all other sts are in stockinette. Approx. every ¾ in / 2 cm, increase 1 st on each side of center st until st count is 78 (80, 82, 84, 84, 88, 90) sts and sleeve is 17¼ (17¾, 17¾, 17¾, 18¼, 18½, 18½) in / 44 (45, 45, 45, 46, 47, 47) cm long or desired length. BO or place on holder the center 7 (9, 11, 13, 13, 15, 17) sts of underarm. Set first sleeve aside while you knit second sleeve the same way.

JOINING/RAGLAN SHAPING

Now it's time to join the body and sleeves on larger circular. Begin with the front and place sleeves at underarms. At each intersection of body and sleeve, pm for raglan shaping = a total of 320 (336, 352, 368, 384, 416, 432) sts. Work around in stockinette for 1¼ (1¼, 1½, ¾, ¾, 1¼, 1¼) in / 3 (3, 4, 2, 2, 3, 3) cm. Now work following Chart **A** for sizes **XS**, **S**, **M**, **L** and Chart **B** for sizes **XL**, **XXL**, **XXXL**. Decrease as shown on the charts.

After completing decreases, 100 (105, 110, 115, 120, 130, 135) sts rem. At center front, place on holder or BO 17 (19, 21, 23, 25, 27, 29) sts for neck. Begin working short rows back and forth and, on every row, at neck edge, set aside or BO

6,4,4,2 (6,4,4,2; 6,4,4,2,2; 6,4,4,2,2,2; 6,4,4,4,2,2,2; 6,4,4,4,2,2,2,2; 6,4,4,4,2,2,2,2,2) sts = a total of 4 (4, 5, 6, 7, 8, 9) short rows. Change to smaller circular and work around in k1, p1 ribbing for 1½ in / 4 cm. BO loosely in ribbing.

FINISHING
Seam underarms. Weave in all ends neatly on WS. Gently steam press pullover under damp pressing cloth.

CHART A

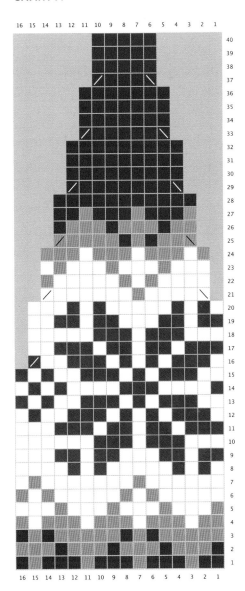

CHART B

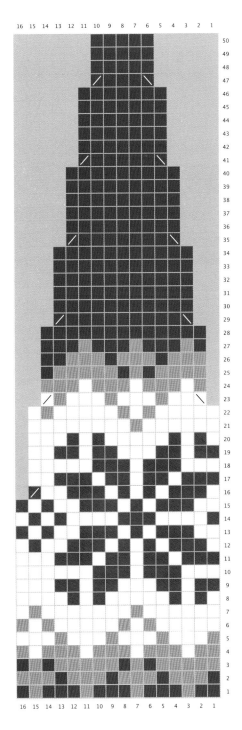

⬜ Sol Natural White 400
⬛ Burgundy-Purple 2132
🟪 Pink 2110
🟫 Dark Brown 2116
╱ K2tog
╲ K2tog tbl or ssk
⬜ White
▨ No st—where sts have been eliminated

SPRUCE PULLOVER

*The Spruce Pullover was inspired by the colors of Norway's evergreen forests—spruce woods—
in winter. On the surface, it may seem gray and quiet, but look more closely and you'll find a
wealth of colors with varied nuances of green, white, brown, and blue.*

||||||||||||||||||||||||||||||||||||||||||||||||||||||||||||||||||||||||

SKILL LEVEL
Experienced

SIZES
XS (S, M, L, XL, XXL)

FINISHED MEASUREMENTS
Chest: approx. 35½ (39½, 43¼, 47¼, 51¼, 55¼) in / 90
(100, 110, 120, 130, 140) cm
Total Length: approx. 23¾ (24½, 25½, 26¾, 27½,
28¼) in / 60 (62, 65, 68, 70, 72) cm
Sleeve Length: approx. 19¾ (19¾, 20, 20, 20½, 20½) in
/ 50 (50, 51, 51, 52, 52) cm

MATERIALS
Yarn:
CYCA #2 (sport, baby) Rauma Finull PT2 (100% Norwe-
gian wool, 191 yd/175 m / 50 g)

Yarn Colors and Amounts:
Olive 476: 200 (250, 300, 300, 350, 350) g
Dark Brown 422: 200 (250, 300, 300, 350, 350) g
Light Gray-Yellow 402: 250 (250, 300, 350, 400, 400) g

Needles:
U. S. sizes 1.5 and 2.5 / 2.5 and 3 mm: circulars and sets
of 5 dpn.
NOTE: If you knit stranded colorwork more firmly than
single-color knitting, you should go up a needle size.

GAUGE
26 sts in stockinette on larger needles = 4 in / 10 cm.
Adjust needle size to obtain correct gauge if necessary.

BODY
With Dark Brown and smaller circular, CO 214
(242, 266, 290, 318, 342) sts. Join, being careful
not to twist cast-on row; pm for beginning of rnd.
Work 20 rnds in k1, p1 ribbing. Change to larger
circular and knit 1 rnd, increasing 22 sts evenly
spaced around = 236 (264, 288, 312, 340, 364) sts.
Pm at each side with 118 (132, 144, 156, 170, 182)
sts each for front and back. **NOTE:** Always purl the
last st at each side as a side st. In order to ensure
that the pattern will be centered with st 1 on front
and back, begin with st 7 (16, 10, 4, 13, 3) of chart.
Work following the chart with the repeat outlined
in red until body measures 16½ (17, 17¼, 18¼,
18½, 19) in / 42 (43, 44, 46, 47, 48) cm or desired
length to underarms. On the last rnd, BO or place
on holders 11 (11, 13, 15, 17, 17) sts centered at
each underarm. Set body aside while you knit the
sleeves.

SLEEVES
With Dark Brown and smaller dpn, CO 56 (58, 60,
62, 64, 66) sts. Divide sts onto dpn and join; pm for
beginning of rnd. Work around in k1, p1 ribbing
for 20 rnds.

Knit 1 rnd. Change to larger dpn. Knit 1 rnd
in Dark Brown and, *at the same time*, increase 6 sts
evenly spaced around = 62 (64, 66, 68, 70, 72) sts.
Always purl the last st (center of underarm) and do
not include it in the pattern. In order to ensure that

BO or place on holder the center 11 (11, 13, 15, 17, 17) sts on underarm. Make sure you end on the same pattern row as for body when ending each sleeve. Set first sleeve aside while you knit second sleeve the same way.

JOINING/RAGLAN SHAPING

Now it's time to join the body and sleeves on larger circular. Pm at each intersection of body and sleeve. Knit 8 (8, 10, 10, 10, 12) rnds in pattern as est. Now you will begin the star pattern on the yoke.

Raglan Shaping: Knit until 3 sts before marker, K2tog, k1, sl m, k1, sl 1, k1, psso (or ssk). **NOTE:** Use whichever is the dominant color on the rnd for the two decreases and the 2 sts on raglan line.

You will decrease at different rates on the body and sleeves. On the body, decrease on every other rnd 16 times and on every rnd 19 (21, 23, 25, 27, 30) times. On the sleeves, decrease on every 4th rnd 4 times, on every other rnd 8 times, and then on every rnd 19 (21, 23, 25, 27, 30) times. After completing star pattern, return to repeat outlined in red.

After all decreases, 144 (160, 168, 176, 188, 204) sts rem. Now work back and forth, continuing raglan decreases as est. At center front, BO or place on holder the center 23 (25, 29, 31, 33, 35) sts. While you knit back and forth following repeat outlined in red, BO or place 8,6,4,2 (8,6,4,2,2; 8,6,4,2,2,2; 8,6,4,4,2,2,2; 8,6,4,4,2,2,2,2; 8,6,4,4,2,2,2,2,2) sts on a holder on each side of front neck. The total st count rem for neckband = 112 (120, 120, 120, 124, 132) sts. Change to smaller circular and work 20 rnds k1, p1 ribbing. BO loosely in ribbing.

FINISHING

Seam underarms. Fold neck band in half and sew down smoothly on WS. Weave in all ends neatly on WS. Gently steam press pullover under damp pressing cloth.

st 1 of chart will be centered on the sleeve, begin with st 3 (2, 1, 16, 15, 14) of chart. Work around following the chart inside the repeat outlined in red. Approx. every ¾ in / 2 cm, increase 1 st on each side of the centered purl st until there are a total of 108 (110, 114, 118, 122, 130) sts.

When sleeve is 19¾ (19¾, 20, 20, 20½, 20½) in / 50 (50, 51, 51, 52, 52) cm long or desired length,

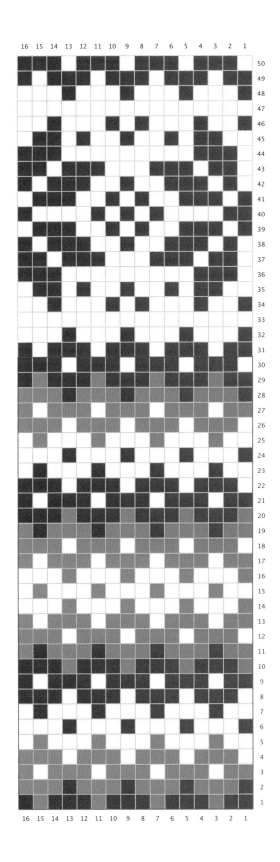

Light Gray-Yellow 402

Dark Brown 422

Olive 476

Repeat for body/sleeves

ÅKLE CARDIGAN

This cardigan was inspired by the pattern motifs and colors in Norway's woven åkle *tapestries. As in the tapestries, several strong colors combine for a harmonic whole.*

‖‖

SKILL LEVEL
Experienced

SIZES
XS (S, M, L, XL, XXL, XXXL)

FINISHED MEASUREMENTS
Chest: approx. 37¾ (40½, 43¾, 47, 50, 52¾, 56) in
/ 96 (103, 111, 119, 127, 134, 142) cm
Total Length: approx. 21¼ (22, 22¾, 23¼, 24½, 24¾,
26) in / 54 (56, 58, 59, 62, 63, 66) cm
Sleeve Length: approx. 19 (19, 19¾, 19¾, 20½, 20½,
20½) in / 48 (48, 50, 50, 52, 52, 52) cm

MATERIALS
Yarn:
CYCA #2 (sport, baby), Rauma Finull PT2 (100% Nor-
wegian wool, 191 yd/175 m / 50 g)

Yarn Colors and Amounts:
Light Gray-Yellow 402: 150 (150, 150, 150, 150, 150,
150) g

Blue-Black 459: 100 (100, 100, 100, 150, 150, 150) g
Ochre 417: 100 (100, 100, 100, 150, 150, 150) g
Moss Green 498: 100 (100, 100, 100, 150, 150, 150) g
Rust Red 419: 100 (100, 100, 100, 150, 150, 150) g

Notions:
6-8 clasp pairs

Needles:
U. S. sizes 1.5 and 2.5 / 2.5 and 3 mm: circulars and
sets of 5 dpn.
NOTE: If you knit stranded colorwork more firmly
than single-color knitting, you should go up a
needle size.

GAUGE
26 sts in stockinette on larger needles = 4 in / 10 cm.
Adjust needle size to obtain correct gauge if
necessary.

BODY
With Light Gray-Yellow and smaller circular, CO
257 (277, 297, 317, 337, 357, 377) sts. Work back
and forth in k1tbl, p1 ribbing for 2 in / 5 cm. On
the last row of ribbing, place the 8 sts on each side
on holders for the front bands = total of 16 sts.

Change to larger circular and knit 1 row, casting on 5 sts between the bands for the steek (steek
sts are not included in subsequent stitch counts.
Now join and knit around following the chart = 241
(261, 281, 301, 321, 341, 361) sts (excluding steek),

or 121 (131, 141, 151, 161, 171, 181) sts for back
and 60 (65, 70, 75, 80, 85, 90) sts for each front.
Pm between each front and back and at beginning
of rnd. In order to ensure that st 3 of chart will be
centered on back, begin with st 3 (1, 3, 1, 3, 1, 3) of
chart. Continue until body measures 15 (15, 15¾,
15¾,16½, 16½, 17¼) in / 38 (38, 40, 40, 42, 42, 44)
cm or desired length to underarms. Centered between each front and the back, BO 10 (10, 12, 12,
14, 14, 16) sts for underarms.

SLEEVES

With Light Gray-Yellow and smaller dpn, CO 54 (54, 60, 60, 60, 64, 64) sts. Divide sts onto dpn and join. Work around in k1tbl, p1 ribbing for 2 in / 5 cm. Change to larger dpn and knit 1 rnd increasing 10 sts evenly spaced around = 64 (64, 70, 70, 70, 74, 74) sts. Now work following the chart. In order to ensure that st 3 of chart will be centered on sleeve, begin with st 4 (4, 1, 1, 1, 3, 3) of chart. **NOTE:** Always purl last st for center of underarm. Use dominant color of rnd for purl st. About every ⅝ in / 1.5 cm, increase 1 st on each side of purl st until there are a total of 106 (110, 114, 118, 122, 126, 130) sts and sleeve is 19 (19, 19¾, 19¾, 20½, 20½, 20½) in / 48 (48, 50, 50, 52, 52, 52) cm long or desired length. Make sure you end on the same pattern row as for body when ending each sleeve. BO or place on holder the center 11 (11, 13, 13, 13, 15, 17) sts of underarm. Set first sleeve aside while you knit second sleeve the same way.

JOINING/RAGLAN SHAPING

Now it's time to join the body and sleeves on larger circular. Knit across front, pm; knit sleeve, pm, knit back, pm, knit sleeve, pm, knit front = total of 411 (439, 459, 487, 511, 535, 555) sts. Work around, without decreasing, following chart for 8 (9, 10, 11, 12, 13, 14) rnds.

Raglan Shaping:

Raglan decreases occur at each marker. You can decide how many sts you want for the raglan lines. On the version shown here, the decreases are placed around a central st, meaning you have a central st with a decrease on each side of it. In that case, knit until 2 sts before central raglan st, k2tog, k1, sl 1, k1, psso (or ssk).

You will decrease at different rates on the body and sleeves. On the front/back, decrease on every other rnd 16 times and on every rnd 23 (27, 30, 33, 37, 40, 43) times.

On the sleeves, decrease on every 4th rnd 4 times, on every other rnd 10 (12, 13, 14, 17, 18, 19) times, and then on every rnd 19 (20, 20, 21, 19, 20, 21) times. After all decreases = 123 (129, 143, 151, 155, 159, 159) sts rem.

FINISHING/FRONT BANDS

Reinforce the steek with crochet or machine stitching (you can find guides for each method on You-Tube). Carefully cut steek open up center st. Place held sts of one band on a smaller needle and CO 8 new sts for a facing to be later sewn down to cover cut steek sts. Work the 8 sts of button band in k1tbl, p1 ribbing as est and work facing sts in stockinette. When band reaches neck, BO the 8 facing sts and place rem ribbing sts onto same needle as rem body sts. Work the opposite front band the same way.

When all rem body and front band sts are on same circular, there are a total of 139 (155, 159, 167, 171, 175, 175) sts. Knit 1 row in Gray-Yellow on smaller circular, *at the same time* decreasing 16 sts evenly spaced across = 123 (123, 127, 135, 135, 143, 143) sts rem. Work 20 rows in k1tbl, p1 ribbing. BO loosely in ribbing. Sew front bands to front edges. Fold facing over cut edges and sew down smoothly on WS. Fold neckband in half and sew down edge to WS. Sew on clasps.

Seam underarms. Weave in all ends neatly on WS. Gently steam press cardigan under damp pressing cloth.

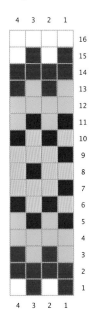

- ☐ Light Gray-Yellow 402
- ■ Blue-Black 459
- ▨ Ochre 417
- ▪ Rust Red 419
- ▫ Moss Green 498

HALF-STAR SLIPPERS

The eight-point star (also called an eight-petal rose) on these slippers is so big that it couldn't fit on one slipper—so I split it up, hence the name half-star slippers. When you stand with your feet together, you'll see one large star on your feet.

IIIIIIIIIIIIIIIIIIIIIIIIIIIIIIIIIIIIIIIIIIIIIIIIIIIIIIIIIIIIIIIIIIIIIII

SKILL LEVEL
Experienced

SIZES
Women's (Men's)

FINISHED MEASUREMENTS
Length: approx. 8 (9½) in / 20 (24) cm
Foot Circumference: approx. 8¾ (10¼) in / 22 (26) cm

MATERIALS
Yarn:
CYCA #1 (fingering) Rauma 2-ply Gammelserie (100% Norwegian wool, 175 yd/160 m / 50 g)

Yarn Colors and Amounts:
Natural White GL401: 50 (50) g
Black GL436: 50 (50) g
Dark Petroleum GL4902: 50 (50) g

Needles:
U. S. sizes 0 and1.5 / 2 and 2.5 mm: sets of 5 dpn.
NOTE: If you knit stranded colorwork more firmly than single-color knitting, you should go up a needle size.

GAUGE
28 sts in stockinette on larger needles = 4 in / 10 cm.
Adjust needle size to obtain correct gauge if necessary.

CASTING ON
The slippers begin with Judy's Magic Cast-on* at the back of the heel: with Natural White and larger dpn, cast-on 3 (5) sts each onto 2 dpn, for a total of 6 (10) sts. With RS facing, k3 (5). K-CO 5 sts following the chart on one side of the cast-on and K-CO 5 sts on opposite side of cast-on.

SLIPPER
Follow Chart **A** (**B**), increasing as indicated on chart (with RLI (an increase leaning right) and LLI for a left-leaning increase) up to the red line on the chart. At the red line, knit the sts with smooth contrast-color scrap yarn, which you will later remove so you can work the ribbing and edging on the slipper. After knitting across with scrap yarn, slide the sts back to left needle and knit those sts in pattern. Continue following the chart, decreasing as shown. Decreases leaning to the right are worked with k2tog and to the left as sl 1, k1, psso (or ssk).

---

* Check YouTube for instructions for Judy's Magic cast-on.

ROLLED EDGE

The slippers have a short rolled edge. With smaller dpn and Dark Petroleum, pick up the sts around the scrap yarn. Carefully remove scrap yarn and knit 1 rnd, picking up and knitting 1 or 2 sts at each corner to avoid holes. On the next rnd, work in k1tbl, p1 ribbing, *at the same time* decreasing evenly spaced around to reduce the stitch count to 62 (72) sts. Work 4 rnds k1 tbl, p1 ribbing and then knit 10 rnds. BO loosely. The edge will roll in after the bind-off.

Weave in all ends neatly on WS. Make the second slipper the same way, reversing shaping/ pattern to match.

CHART A

	Natural White GL 401
■	Black GL436
	scrap yarn
/	K2tog
\	Sl 1, k1 psso or ssk
Ⲕ	RLI
Ⲩ	LLI

CHART B

ROSE SOCKS

These rose socks are different from the other patterns in the book because the motif is organic rather than geometric. The design is more inspired by a typical embroidery pattern, used here to make a rose pattern to climb up the leg.

IIIIIIIIIIIIIIIIIIIIIIIIIIIIIIIIIIIIIIIIIIIIIIIIIIIIIIIIIIIIIIIIIIIIIIIIIIIII

SKILL LEVEL
Experienced

SIZES
Women's (Men's)

FINISHED MEASUREMENTS
Leg Length: approx. 5¼ (6¾) in / 13 (17) cm
Foot Length: approx. 8 (10¼) in / 20 (26) cm

MATERIALS
Yarn:
CYCA #1 (fingering) Rauma 2-ply Gammelserie (100% Norwegian wool, 175 yd/160 m / 50 g)

Yarn Colors and Amounts:
Natural White GL401: 50 (50) g
Burgundy GL4901: 50 (100) g

Needles:
U. S. sizes 0 and 1.5 / 2 and 2.5 mm: sets of 5 dpn
NOTE: If you knit stranded colorwork more firmly than single-color knitting, you should go up a needle size.

GAUGE
26 sts in stockinette on larger needles = 4 in / 10 cm.
Adjust needle size to obtain correct gauge if necessary.

RIBBING
With Burgundy and smaller dpn, CO 52 (72) sts. Divide sts onto dpn and join. Work 4 rnds k1tbl, p1 ribbing. With Natural White, knit 1 rnd, increasing 8 sts evenly spaced around = 60 (80) sts,

LEG
Change to larger dpn and work in pattern following Chart **A** (**B**) until you've worked 3 (4) roses in length or leg measure 5¼ (6¾) in / 13 (17) cm. Now k29 (39) with smooth, contrast-color scrap yarn on back of sock. The scrap yarn will be removed later to release sts for the heel.

FOOT
After you've knitted in the scrap yarn, slide those sts back to left needle and knit them following charted pattern. Continue in pattern until you've worked 3 (4) roses in length or to desired length before toe.

TOE/HEEL
Work both the toe and heel in Burgundy.
Toe: On the first rnd, decrease as follows; 30 (40) sts each for instep and sole.
Ndls 1 and 3: K2, ssk, knit to end of needle.
Ndls 2 and 4: Knit until 3 sts rem, k2tog, k1.

Decrease the same way until 4 sts rem. Cut yarn and draw end through rem sts; tighten.

HEEL

Insert a dpn through sts in row below scrap yarn and a second dpn through sts above scrap yarn. Carefully remove scrap yarn.

With larger dpn and Burgundy, knit 1 rnd with out decreasing. If you have a high instep, knit a few extra rnds. Now decrease as for toe.

Weave in all ends neatly on WS. Make the second sock the same way, reversing chart pattern to match.

CHART A

☐ Natural White GL401

■ Burgundy GL4901

CHART B

SNOWSTORM SOCKS

These classic and rather old-fashioned snowstorm socks are based on a simple pattern repeat. The name derives from the small "lice" between the little Selbu roses, which also make the socks a good beginner's project.

||||||||||||||||||||||||||||||||||||||||||||||||||||||||||||||||||||||||

SKILL LEVEL
Experienced

SIZES
Women's (Men's)

FINISHED MEASUREMENTS
Leg Length: approx. 5½ (6¾) in / 14 (17) cm
Foot Length: approx. 8 (10¾) in / 20 (27) cm

MATERIALS
Yarn:
CYCA #1 (fingering) Trollkar Slitesterk (80% soft wool, 20% polyester, approx. 383 yd/350 m / 100 g)

Yarn Colors and Amounts:
Light Gray 910: 100 (100) g
Charcoal Gray 995: 100 (100) g

Needles:
U. S. sizes 0 and 2.5 / 2 and 3 mm: sets of 5 dpn

GAUGE
26 sts in stockinette on larger needles = 4 in / 10 cm.
Adjust needle size to obtain correct gauge if necessary.
NOTE: You can adjust the size of the socks by changing your needle size. For example, if you want a smaller size, you can follow the chart for the smaller size using U. S. 0 / 2 mm needles for the ribbing and U.S. 1.5 / 2.5 mm for the pattern.

RIBBING
With Light Gray and smaller dpn, CO 52 (72) sts. Divide sts onto dpn and join. Work 4 rnds k1tbl, p1 ribbing. Knit 1 rnd, increasing 8 sts evenly spaced around = 60 (80) sts.

LEG
Change to larger dpn and work in pattern following chart for 5½ (6¾) in / 14 (17) cm or desired length. On Row 1 or 11 of chart, k29 (39) with smooth, contrast-color scrap yarn on back of sock. The scrap yarn will be removed later to release sts for the heel.

After you've knitted in the scrap yarn, slide those sts back to left needle and knit them following charted pattern.

FOOT
Continue in pattern until you've worked 5½ (6¾) in / 14 (17) cm after scrap yarn, or to desired length before toe.

TOE/HEEL
Work both the toe and heel in Charcoal Gray.
Toe: On the first rnd, decrease as follows; 30 (40) sts each for instep and sole.
Ndls 1 and 3: K1, ssk, knit to end of needle.
Ndls 2 and 4: Knit until 3 sts rem, k2tog, k1.

Decrease the same way until 4 sts rem. Cut yarn and draw end through rem sts; tighten.

HEEL

Insert a dpn through sts in row below scrap yarn and a second dpn through sts above scrap yarn. Carefully remove scrap yarn.

With larger dpn and Charcoal Gray, knit 1 rnd without decreasing. If you have a high instep, knit a few extra rnds. Now decrease as for toe.

Weave in all ends neatly on WS. Make the second sock the same way.

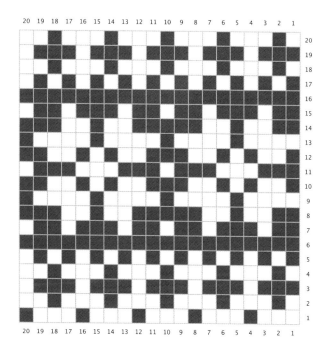

□ Light Gray 910
■ Charcoal Gray 995

HENPECKED SLIPPERS

The phrase "henpecked husband" (the English equivalent to the idiom "slipper hero"—tøffelhelt—in Norwegian) is often used disparagingly if a husband lets himself be nagged and bossed around. In Norwegian, to be "under the slipper" is applied in the same way to a wife. Today, fortunately, we have a more equal society and such expressions lose both their power and their sarcasm. Now they're just fun names for slippers!

||||||||||||||||||||||||||||||||||||||||||||||||||||||||||||||||||||||||

SKILL LEVEL
Experienced

SIZES
Women's (Men's)

FINISHED MEASUREMENTS
Length: approx. 8¾ (11¾) in / 22 (30) cm
Foot Circumference: approx. 8 (9½) in / 20 (24) cm

MATERIALS
Yarn:
CYCA #3 (DK, light worsted) Hillesvåg Fjord Sokkegarn 2 (80% Norwegian wool, 20% nylon, 273 yd/250 m / 100 g)

Yarn Colors and Amounts:
Dark Green 03510 (Ochre Yellow 03526): 100 (100) g
Bleached White 03504: 100 (100) g
Black 035112: 100 (100) g

Needles:
U. S. size 4 / 3.5 mm: set of 5 dpn.
NOTE: To adjust the slipper size, go up or down a needle size.

GAUGE
24 sts in pattern = 4 in / 10 cm.
Adjust needle size to obtain correct gauge if necessary.

CASTING ON

With Dark Green (Ochre Yellow), CO 44 (60) sts. Divide sts onto dpn and join. Work 10 rnds in k1, p1 ribbing. Knit 1 rnd, purl 1 rnd, knit 11 rnds. On the last rnd, increase 4 (6) sts evenly spaced around = 48 (66) sts.

HEEL

Work back and forth over the first 23 (29) sts. Follow Chart **A** (**A***); the st column outlined with red is the center st of heel flap. The chart pattern mirror-images around the center st. The heel flap is symmetrical, with one eight-petal rose on each side of the center st.

After the last row of Chart **A** (**A***), *work in pattern following Chart **B** until 3 sts past the center st of heel. K2tog, k1. Turn and sl 1, purl until 3 sts past center st, p2tog, p1. Rep from *, working back and forth until all the heel sts have been worked.

FOOT

Knit to the "edge" of heel flap from right side. When you come to the flap, pick up and knit 7 (9) sts along edge in Chart **B** pattern. On instep, follow Chart **C** (**C***). Begin at lower right corner of chart. Next, pick up and knit 7 (9) sts along opposite edge of heel flap in Chart **B** pattern. Continue knitting around following Chart **B** for sole and Chart **C** (**C***) for instep.

CHART A

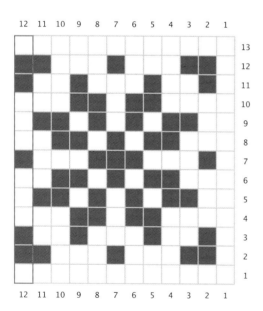

CHART A*

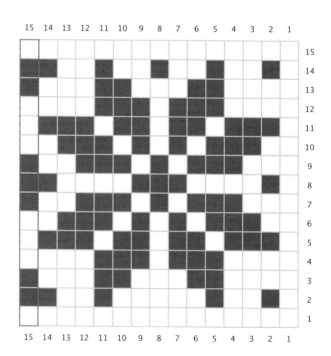

Decrease on sole for gusset until 19 (25) sts rem on sole: On every other rnd, work sole following Chart **B** until 2 sts before Chart **C** (**C***)/instep, k2tog. After Chart **C** (**C***)/instep, ssk and knit as est to end of rnd (center of sole). Continue decreasing the same way on alternate rnds until 44 (60) sts rem.

Shape toe on both sole and instep as indicated on Chart **C** (**C***).

Weave in all ends neatly on WS. Make the second slipper the same way.

CHART B

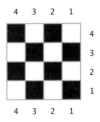

CHART C

	Bleached White 03504
■	Black 03511
╱	K2tog
╲	Ssk or sl 1, k1, psso
▓	No stitch

CHART C*

Bleached White 03504

Black 03511

/ K2tog

\ Ssk or sl 1, k1, psso

No stitch

ÅKLE SOCKS AND SLIPPERS

If you look at an åkle tapestry and at knitted fabric, you will discover that they have several similarities in terms of pattern type. Both are embellished by the possibilities inherent in the technique—especially, first and foremost, geometric motifs. Here a simple åkle-inspired pattern is repeated over an entire sock.

SIZES
Women's (Men's)

FINISHED MEASUREMENTS
Leg Length: approx. 6 (7½) in / 15 (19) cm
Foot Length: approx. 9 (11½) in / 23 (29) cm

MATERIALS
Yarn:
CYCA #1 (fingering) Sandnes Garn Sisu (80% wool, 20% nylon, approx. 191 yd/175 m / 50 g)

Yarn Colors and Amounts:
Suggestion 1:
White 1001: 50 (50) g
Gray Heather 1042: 50 (50) g
Charcoal Heather 1088: 50 (50) g
Old Rose 4513: 50 (50) g

Suggestion 2:
White 1001: 50 (50) g
Gray Blue 5962: 50 (50) g
Dusty Green 7243: 50 (50) g
Orange 3326: 50 (50) g

Needles:
U. S. sizes 0 and 2.5 / 2 and 3 mm: sets of 5 dpn

GAUGE
27 sts in stockinette on larger needles = 4 in / 10 cm.
Adjust needle size to obtain correct gauge if necessary.

CASTING ON AND RIBBING

With smaller dpn and Gray Heather (White), CO 52 (72) sts. Divide sts onto dpn and join. Work 4 rnds k1tbl, p1 ribbing.

LEG

The rnd begins on the inside of the leg (to hide the break or jog in the pattern when you change rnds). Knit 1 rnd, increasing 8 sts evenly spaced around = 60 (80) sts. Change to larger dpn and work in pattern with Color Suggestion 1 (2) following chart. Rep pattern sequence 4 (5) times in length.

HEEL

K29 (39) with smooth, contrast-color scrap yarn on back of sock. The scrap yarn will be removed later to release sts for the heel. After you've knitted in the scrap yarn, slide those sts back to left needle and knit them following charted pattern.

FOOT

Continue in pattern, repeating pattern 4 (5) times in length.

TOE/HEEL

Work the toe in Gray Heather (White).
Toe:
Ndls 1 and 3: K1, ssk, knit to end of needle.
Ndls 2 and 4: Knit until 3 sts rem, k2tog, k1.
Decrease the same way on every rnd until 8 sts rem. Cut yarn and draw end through rem sts; tighten.

HEEL

Insert a dpn through sts in row below scrap yarn and a second dpn through sts above scrap yarn. Carefully remove scrap yarn.

With larger dpn and Gray Heather (White), knit 1 rnd without decreasing. If you have a high instep, knit a few extra rnds. Now decrease as for toe.

Weave in all ends neatly on WS. Make the second sock the same way.

ÅKLE SLIPPERS

Work as for *Åkle* Socks but with only 1 pattern rep in length on leg for both sizes. After completing leg, continue as for socks.

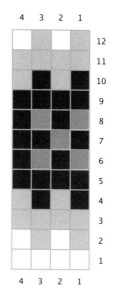

COLOR SUGGESTION 1:

White 1001

Gray Heather 1042

Charcoal Heather 1088

Old Rose 4513

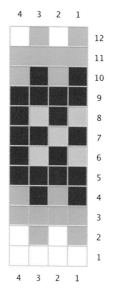

COLOR SUGGESTION 2:

White 1001

Gray Blue 5962

Dusty Green 7243

Orange 3326

STAR COWL

Cowls are a perfect beginner's project precisely because they don't involve any complicated shaping or fiddly details. This star cowl is also a good beginner's project for anyone not experienced with two-color stranded knitting because the pattern is geometric and easy to memorize. If you have the desire and patience, you can also extend it to make a nice scarf.

‖‖

SKILL LEVEL
Experienced

SIZES
S (L)

FINISHED MEASUREMENTS
Circumference: approx. 20 (26¾) in / 51 (68) cm
Total Length: approx. 12½ (12½) in / 31.5 (31.5) cm

MATERIALS
Yarn:
CYCA #2 (sport, baby) Rauma Finull PT2 (100% Norwegian wool, 191 yd/175 m / 50 g)

Yarn Colors and Amounts:
Brown Heather 464: 50 (50) g
Camel 4077: 50 (50) g

Needles:
U. S. sizes 1.5 and 2.5 / 2.5 and 3 mm: circular 24 in / 60 cm
NOTE: If you knit stranded colorwork more firmly than single-color knitting, you should go up a needle size.

GAUGE
26 sts in stockinette on larger needles = 4 in / 10 cm.
Adjust needle size to obtain correct gauge if necessary.

CASTING ON

With Brown Heather and smaller circular, CO 120 (164) sts. Join, being careful not to twist cast-on row; pm for beginning of rnd. Work 4 rnds in k2, p2 ribbing. Change to larger circular and knit 1 rnd, increasing 12 sts evenly spaced around = 132 (176) sts. Now continue in charted pattern on page 58 until cowl is 11¾ in / 30 cm high or desired length.

BINDING OFF

Knit 1 rnd, changing to smaller circular and *at the same time* decreasing 12 sts evenly spaced around = 120 (164) sts rem. Work 4 rnds in k2, p2 ribbing. BO loosely in ribbing.

FINISHING

Weave in all ends neatly on WS. Gently steam press cowl under a damp pressing cloth.

STAR SCARF

|||||||||||||||||||||||||||||||||||||||||||||||||||||||||||||||||||||||||||||||||||||||||||||||||||||||||||||||

SKILL LEVEL
Experienced

FINISHED MEASUREMENTS
Total Length: approx. 63 (70¾) in / 160 (180) cm

MATERIALS
Yarn:
CYCA #2 (sport, baby) Rauma Finull PT2 (100% Norwegian wool, 191 yd/175 m / 50 g)

Yarn Colors and Amounts:
Charcoal Heather 414: 150 (150) g
White 400: 150 (150) g

Needles:
U. S. sizes 1.5 and 2.5 / 2.5 and 3 mm: circular 24 in / 60 cm
NOTE: If you knit stranded colorwork more firmly than single-color knitting, you should go up a needle size.

GAUGE
26 sts in stockinette on larger needles = 4 in / 10 cm. Adjust needle size to obtain correct gauge If necessary.

If you want a nice warm scarf, simply follow the instructions for the Star Cowl and continue until it is 63 (70¾) in / 160 (180) cm long. Seam each end for a flat, double layer scarf.

☐ Camel 4077 / White 400

■ Brown Heather 464 / Charcoal Heather 414

RUST COWL

Pelsull yarn from Hillesvåg Ullvarefabrikk is soft and lustrous, with a special heathered look obtained by overdyeing its natural shades of gray. This simple cowl is enhanced by lovely shades and colors that remind me of rust on metal. You can choose from three sizes depending on whether you want a tight or loose fit.

|||||||||||||||||||||||||||||||||||||||||||||||||||||||||||||||||||||||||||||||

SKILL LEVEL
Experienced

SIZES
S (M, L)

FINISHED MEASUREMENTS
Circumference: approx. 20 (25½, 31½) in / 51 (65, 80) cm
Total Length: approx. 11¾ in / 30 cm for all 3 sizes

MATERIALS
Yarn:
CYCA #3 (DK, light worsted) Hillesvåg Ullvarefabrikk Tinde pelsullgarn (100% Norwegian wool, 284 yd/ 260 m / 100 g)

Yarn Colors and Amounts:
Cognac 2103: 100 (150, 200) g
Natural Gray 2115: 100 (150, 200) g

Needles:
U. S. sizes 2.5 and 6 / 3 and 4 mm: circular
NOTE: If you knit stranded colorwork more firmly than single-color knitting, you should go up a needle size.

GAUGE
22 sts in stockinette on larger needles = 4 in / 10 cm.
Adjust needle size to obtain correct gauge if necessary.

CASTING ON
With Natural Gray and smaller circular, CO 112 (144, 176) sts. Join, being careful not to twist cast-on row; pm for beginning of rnd. Knit 1 rnd; turn so the wrong side is now knitted. Work 3 rnds in k1 Cognac, p1 Natural Gray ribbing.

NECK
Change to larger circular and work around in charted pattern until cowl is approx. 10¾ in / 27 cm from cast-on edge or desired length.

BINDING OFF
Change to smaller circular. Work 3 rnds in k1 Cognac, p1 Natural Gray ribbing. For the last rnd, knit on WS with Natural Gray (to match beginning of cowl). BO loosely.

FINISHING
Weave in all ends neatly on WS. Gently steam press cowl under a damp pressing cloth.

61

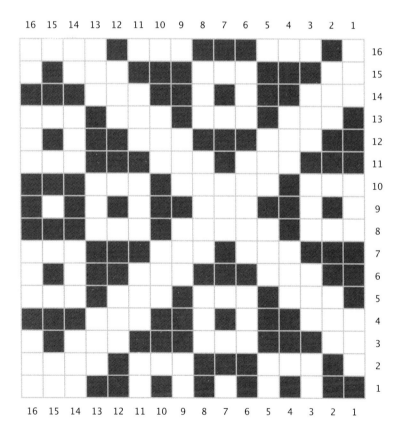

Natural Gray 2115																
Cognac 2103																

KROKBRAGD SCARF OR COWL

*The pattern on this scarf reminds me of Norwegian **krokbragd** weaving (3-shaft, weft-faced pointed twill), hence the name. The scarf is knitted in the round, so it'll be especially warm around your neck.*

||||||||||||||||||||||||||||||||||||||||||||||||||||||||||||||||||

SKILL LEVEL
Experienced

FINISHED MEASUREMENTS
Width: approx. 11 in / 28 cm
Total Length: approx. 70¾ in / 180 cm

MATERIALS
Yarn:
CYCA #3 (DK, light worsted) Hillesvåg Ullvarefabrikk Tinde pelsullgarn (100% Norwegian wool, 284 yd/ 260 m / 100 g)

Yarn Colors and Amounts:
Scarf
Cognac 2103: 200 g
Dark Brown 2116: 200 g
Burgundy 2104: 200 g

Cowl
Cognac 2103: 100 g
Dark Brown 2116: 100 g
Burgundy 2104: 100 g

Needles:
U. S. size 4 / 3.5 mm: circular
NOTE: If you knit stranded colorwork more firmly than single-color knitting, you should go up a needle size.

GAUGE
22 sts in stockinette on larger needles = 4 in / 10 cm. Adjust needle size to obtain correct gauge if necessary.

INSTRUCTIONS
With Cognac and circular, CO 128 sts. Join, being careful not to twist cast-on row; pm for beginning of rnd. Knit 1 rnd with Cognac and then work from charted pattern until scarf is approx. 70¾ in / 180 cm long or desired length. BO with Cognac.

FINISHING
Seam each end for a flat double-layered scarf. Cut lengths of yarn for fringe. With a strand of each color in each fringe, use a large, blunt tapestry needle to tie fringe along each sewn edge.

Weave in all ends neatly on WS. Gently steam press scarf under a damp pressing cloth.

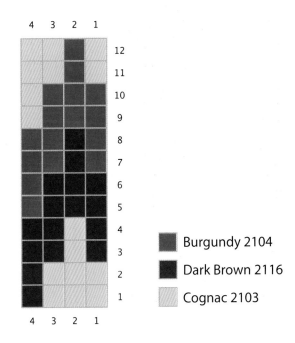

COWL

If you prefer, you can bind off the scarf when it is approx. 11¾ in / 30 cm long to make a loose cowl or work as follows. CO 118 sts and join to work in the round. Work 3 rnds k1, p1 ribbing. Knit 1 rnd with Cognac, increasing 10 sts evenly spaced around to 128 sts. Work as for scarf until cowl is 11¾ in / 30 cm high. Knit 1 rnd, decreasing 10 sts evenly spaced around to 118 sts. Work 3 rnds k1, p1 ribbing and then BO loosely in ribbing.

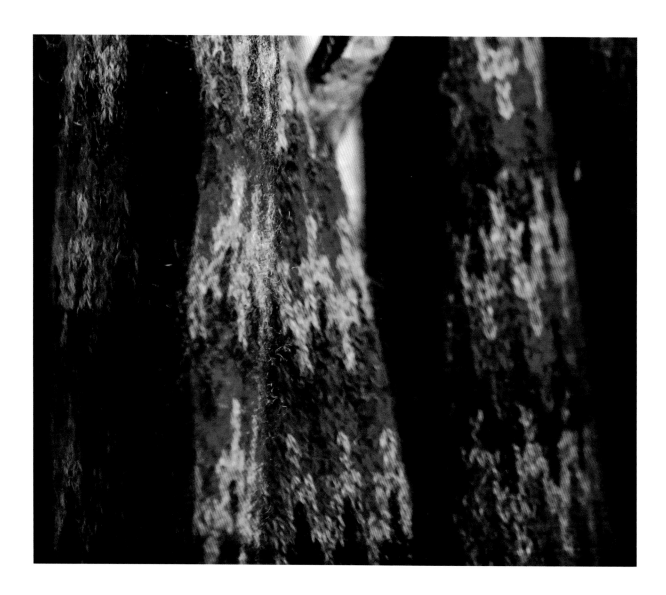

CABLE SCARF

Although the Aran Islands, off the west coast of Ireland, are the most strongly associated with cable knitting traditions, Norway also has a rich history involving cabling, particularly on stockings for folk costumes. This cabled scarf was inspired by that tradition.

||||||||||||||||||||||||||||||||||||||||||||||||||||||||||||||

SKILL LEVEL
Experienced

FINISHED MEASUREMENTS
Width: approx. 13 in / 33 cm
Total Length: approx. 70¾ in / 180 cm

MATERIALS
Yarn:
CYCA #2 (sport, baby), Hillesvåg Ullvarefabrikk Ask (100% Norwegian wool, 344 yd/315 m / 100 g)

Yarn Color and Amount:
Brass Yellow 6092: 300 g

Needles:
U. S. size 4 / 3.5 mm: circular or straight; cable needle

GAUGE
30 sts in cable pattern = 4 in / 10 cm.
Adjust needle size to obtain correct gauge if necessary.
NOTE: Cable knitting tends to draw the fabric in, so the stitch count is higher than for a corresponding finished piece worked in stockinette. Because the gauge is tighter than normal for Ask yarn, if you go up in needle size, the dimensions (especially the width) of the scarf will increase.

INSTRUCTIONS
CO 100 sts. Knit 10 rows back and forth = 5 ridges.

CABLES
Now work charted cable pattern, beginning with Row 1 of chart, until scarf is approx. 70¾ in / 180 cm long or desired length.

FINISHING
Knit 10 rows (5 ridges) and then BO. Weave in all ends neatly on WS.

CHART FOR CABLE SCARF

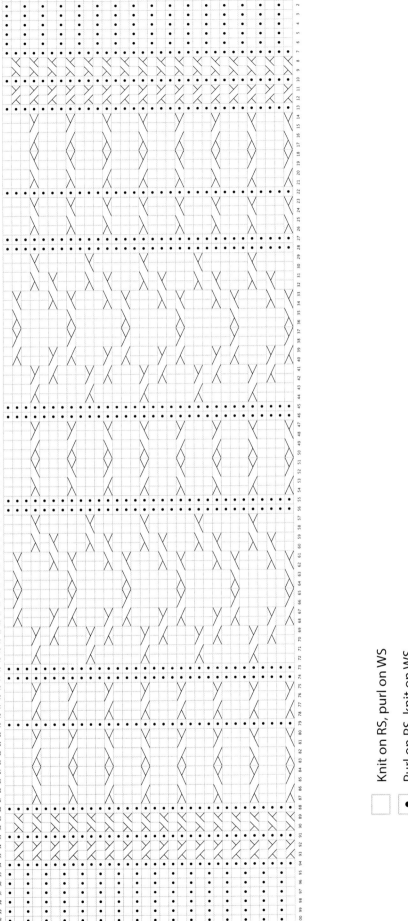

Knit on RS, purl on WS

• Purl on RS, knit on WS

Place 1 st on cable needle and hold in back of work; k1 from left needle and then k1 from cable needle.

Place 1 st on cable needle and hold in front of work; k1 from left needle and then k1 from cable needle.

Place 2 sts on cable needle and hold in back of work; k2 from left needle and then k2 from cable needle.

Place 2 sts on cable needle and hold in front of work; k2 from left needle and then k2 from cable needle.

CLOVER FINGERLESS GLOVES

I named the pattern for these fingerless gloves Clover after the little clover panel on the cuffs. This style of glove is just right for areas of Norway where the spring weather is cheerful but still a little chilly. The green color was chosen to emphasize the springtime feeling in this organic pattern.

SKILL LEVEL
Experienced

SIZE
One size fits all

FINISHED MEASUREMENTS
Circumference: approx. 11 in / 28 cm
Total Length: approx. 7 in / 17.5 cm

MATERIALS
Yarn:
CYCA #1 (fingering) Rauma 2-ply Gammelserie (100% Norwegian wool, 175 yd/160 m / 50 g)

Yarn Colors and Amounts:
White GL 400: 50 g
Dark Olive GL476: 50 g

Needles:
U. S. sizes 0 and 1.5 / 2 and 2.5 mm: sets of 5 dpn.
NOTE: If you knit stranded colorwork more firmly than single-color knitting, you should go up a needle size.

GAUGE
28 sts in pattern on larger needles = 4 in / 10 cm.
Adjust needle size to obtain correct gauge if necessary.

SEED STITCH
Worked across a multiple of 2 sts.
Rnd 1: (K1, p1) around.
Rnd 2: (P1, k1) around.
Rep Rnds 1-2.

CUFF
With Dark Olive and smaller dpn, CO 54 sts. Divide sts onto dpn and join. Work 4 rnds in seed st. Change to larger dpn and White. Knit 1 rnd, increasing 6 sts evenly spaced around = 60 sts. Work in pattern following Chart **A**.

HAND
Knit 1 rnd with White, increasing 6 sts evenly spaced around = 66 sts. Work following Chart **B**, increasing for thumb gusset as shown on the chart. Work RLI for right-leaning decreases and LLI for left-leaning. At the red line on the chart, knit those sts with smooth, contrast-color scrap yarn, which you will later remove. Slide the st back to left needle and knit in pattern. Alternatively, you can place the thumb sts on a holder and CO the same number of sts over the gap. Continue following Chart **B** until completed. Change to smaller dpn and knit 2 rnds with White, decreasing 6 sts evenly spaced around = 60 sts rem. Finish with Olive Green: Knit 1 rnd and then work 4 rnds seed st. BO in seed st.

Make left-hand glove the same way, placing thumb gusset on left side of palm.

THUMB

Worked on larger dpn. Insert a dpn through sts below scrap yarn and another dpn through sts above
scrap yarn. Carefully remove scrap yarn. Or, knit
live held sts and pick up and knit same number of
sts along cast-on row of thumbhole. To avoid holes,
pick up and knit 1 extra st at each corner and then
decrease them away on the next rnd = 30 sts for
thumb.

Work following Chart **C**. After the last rnd,
knit 1 rnd with Dark Olive, decreasing 2 sts evenly

spaced around = 28 sts rem. Work 3 rnds k1, p1
ribbing and then BO in ribbing. Weave in all ends
neatly on WS.

CHART A

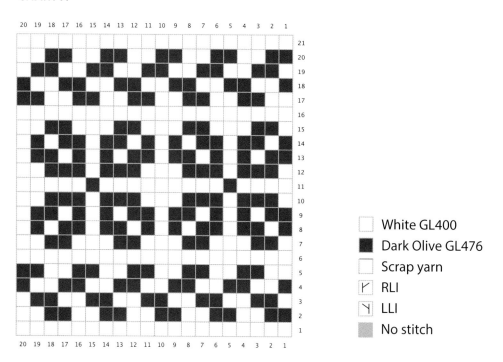

☐ White GL400
■ Dark Olive GL476
☐ Scrap yarn
⌐ RLI
⌐ LLI
▨ No stitch

CHART C

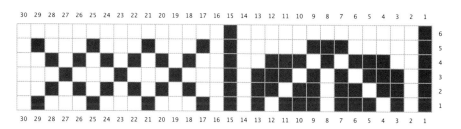

CHART B

SNOWSTORM MITTENS AND FINGERLESS GLOVES

The small lice scattered between the large motifs on these mitts imitate snowflakes falling on mittens during a storm. In many ways, this design is typical of how, when sketching a pattern, I add small elements to avoid large floats on the wrong side.

‖‖

SKILL LEVEL
Experienced

SIZES
Women's (Men's)

FINISHED MEASUREMENTS
Mittens
Circumference: approx. 8¾ (10¾) in / 22 (27) cm
Total Length: approx. 9¾ (10¼) in / 25 (26) cm
Fingerless Gloves
Circumference: approx. 8¾ (10¾) in / 22 (27) cm
Total Length: approx. 6¾ (7) in / 17 (18) cm

MATERIALS
Yarn:
CYCA #1 (fingering) Rauma 2-ply Gammelserie (100% Norwegian wool, 175 yd/160 m / 50 g)

Yarn Colors and Amounts:
Mittens or Fingerless Gloves, one pair
White GL 400: 50 (50) g
Blue GL447: 50 (50) g

Needles:
U. S. sizes 0 and 1.5 / 2 and 2.5 mm: sets of 5 dpn; cable needle for women's version.
NOTE: If you knit stranded colorwork more firmly than single-color knitting, you should go up a needle size.

GAUGE
28 sts in pattern on larger needles = 4 in / 10 cm.
Adjust needle size to obtain correct gauge if necessary.

WOMEN'S CABLE CUFF

With White and smaller dpn, CO 48 sts. Divide sts onto dpn and join. Purl 1 rnd. Now work around in cable pattern:
Rnds 1-3: Work (p2, k4) around.
Rnd 4: *P2, place 2 sts on cable needle and hold in front of work, k2, k2 from cable needle*. Rep * to * around.
Rep Rnd 1-4 6 more times = 28 cable rnds.

MEN'S CUFF

With White and smaller dpn, CO 54 sts. Divide sts onto dpn and join. Work 4 rnds, k1, p1 ribbing. Change to larger dpn and knit 1 rnd, increasing 6 sts evenly spaced around = 60 sts. Work following Chart **A**.

MITTEN HAND

Knit 1 rnd with White, increasing 6 (7) sts evenly spaced around = 54 (67) sts. Work around following Chart **B** (**C**), increasing for thumb gusset as shown on the chart.

At the red line above gusset on the chart, knit those sts with smooth, contrast-color scrap yarn, which you will later remove. Slide the st back to left needle and knit in pattern. Alternatively, you can place the thumb sts on a holder and CO the same number of sts over the gap.

Continue following Chart **B** (**C**) decreasing with k2tog at side as shown on chart. Continue to top shaping. Decrease with k2tog for right-leaning decreases and with ssk or sl 1, k1, psso for left-leaning. When 6 (10) sts rem (= side bands), join bands with Kitchener st for a smooth finish or cut yarn and draw through rem sts; tighten.

Make left-hand mitten the same way, placing thumb gusset on left side of palm.

THUMB

Worked on larger dpn. Insert a dpn through sts below scrap yarn and another dpn through sts above scrap yarn. Carefully remove scrap yarn. Or, knit live held sts and pick up and knit same number of sts along cast-on row of thumbhole. To avoid holes, pick up and knit 1 extra st at each corner = 28 (32) sts for thumb.

Work following Chart **D** (**E**). Shape and finish top as for top of mitten.

Weave in all ends neatly on WS.

FINGERLESS GLOVES

If you prefer fingerless gloves, work as for mittens, ending at the red line on the back of hand on Chart **B** (**C**). Knit 1 rnd with White, decreasing 7 sts evenly spaced around = 55 (70) sts rem. Work 3 rnds k1, p1 ribbing and then BO in ribbing.

Work thumb as for mittens, ending at red line across front and back of thumb on Chart **D** (**E**). Knit 1 rnd with White, decreasing evenly spaced around to 24 (28) sts. Work 3 rnds k1, p1 ribbing and then BO in ribbing.

Weave in all ends neatly on WS.

CHART D

White GL400

Blue GL447

Scrap yarn (fingerless version)

K2tog

Ssk or sl 1, k1, psso

LLI

RLI

CHART B

	White GL400		/	K2tog
■	Blue GL447		\	Ssk or sl 1, k1, psso
	Scrap yarn (fingerless version)		Ⱶ	LLI
			Ⱶ	RLI

CHART C

CHART A

CHART E

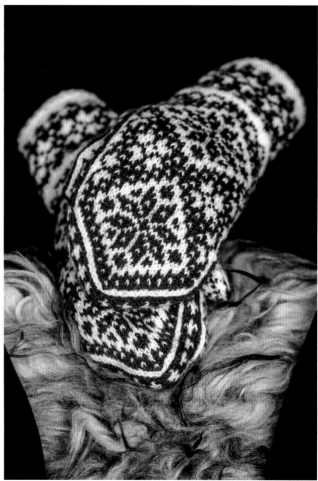

HALF-STAR MITTENS

The eight-petal rose (or eight-point star) has had a number of different names, depending on how many stitches were in the rose. Small roses with two or three "petals" would be two- and three-petal roses, while a large eight-petal rose might a "fourteen-petal rose."* In this design, there are 16 stitches on the men's mittens, so it would be a "sixteen-point star." The star's too big for one mitten, and has been split with one half on each mitten—so, of course, these are named "Half-Star Mittens."

MEN'S MITTENS

SKILL LEVEL
Experienced

SIZE
Men's

FINISHED MEASUREMENTS
Circumference: approx. 10¾ in / 27 cm
Total Length: approx. 11½ in / 29 cm

MATERIALS
Yarn:
CYCA #2 (sport, baby) Lofoten Wool Snykvit 2-ply (100% pure Norwegian wool, 344 yd/315 m / 100 g)
CYCA #2 (sport, baby) Lofoten Wool Skarv 2-ply (100% pure Norwegian wool, 344 yd/315 m / 100 g)

Alternate Yarn Suggestion:
CYCA #1 (fingering) Rauma 2-ply Gammelserie (100% Norwegian wool, 175 yd/160 m / 50 g)

Yarn Colors and Amounts:
Snykvit (white): 100 g
Skarv (black): 100 g

Needles:
U. S. sizes 0 and 1.5 / 2 and 2.5 mm: sets of 5 dpn.

GAUGE
28 sts in pattern on larger needles = 4 in / 10 cm.
Adjust needle size to obtain correct gauge if necessary.

CUFF
With White and smaller dpn, CO 52 sts. Divide sts onto dpn and join. Work 3 rnds k1 tbl, p1 ribbing. Change to larger dpn and knit 1 rnd, increasing 8 sts evenly spaced around = 60 sts. Work following Chart **A** for cuff = pattern section outlined in red.

MITTEN HAND
Continue following Chart **A**. Knit 1 rnd increasing 6 sts evenly spaced around = 66 sts. Now work hand on Chart **A**, increasing for thumb gusset as shown on the chart. Increase with RLI for right-leaning increases and LLI for left-leaning.

At the red line above gusset on the chart, knit sts with smooth, contrast-color scrap yarn, which you will later remove. Slide the st back to left needle and knit in pattern. Alternatively, you can place the thumb sts on a holder and CO the same number of sts over the gap. Continue to top shaping. Decrease with k2tog for right-leaning decreases and with ssk or sl 1, k1, psso for left-leaning. When 16 sts rem, join sides with Kitchener st for a smooth finish or cut yarn and draw through rem sts; tighten.

---

* Anne Bårdsgård, *Selbu Mittens*, Trafalgar Square Books, 2019

THUMB

Worked on larger dpn. Insert a dpn through sts below scrap yarn and another dpn through sts above scrap yarn. Carefully remove scrap yarn. Or, knit live held sts and pick up and knit same number of sts along cast-on row of thumbhole. To avoid holes, pick up and knit 1 extra st at each corner = 32 sts for thumb.

Work following Chart **B**. Shape and finish top as for top of mitten.

Weave in all ends neatly on WS. Make left-hand mitten the same way, mirror-imaging charts so the pair will show a large eight-petal rose when held together. Don't forget to place left thumb on left side of palm.

CHART B

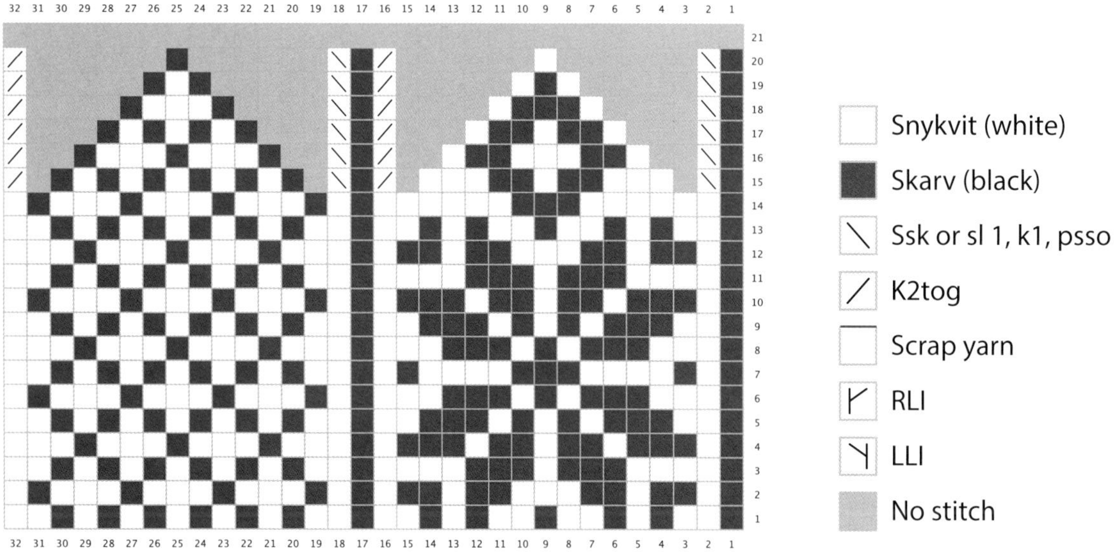
Snykvit (white)
Skarv (black)
Ssk or sl 1, k1, psso
K2tog
Scrap yarn
RLI
LLI
No stitch

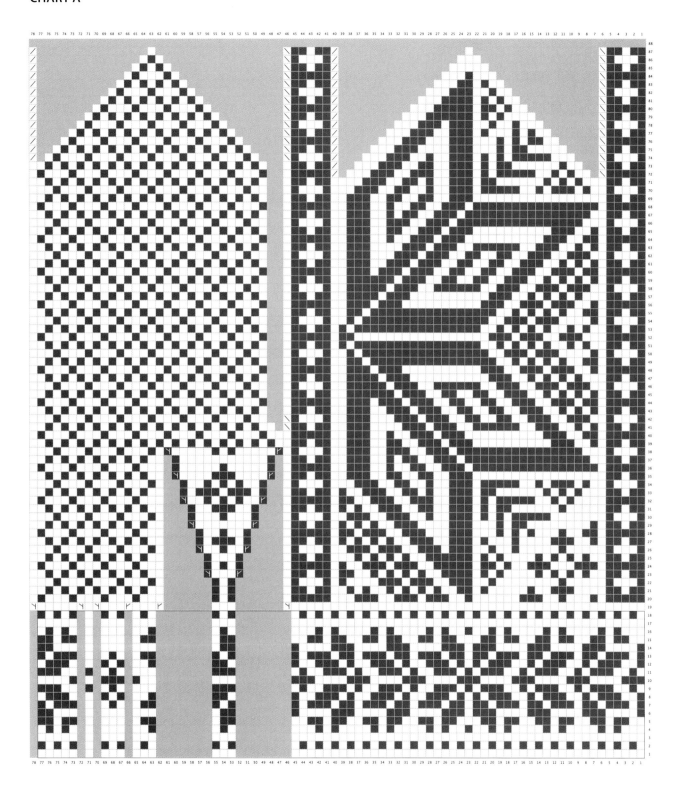

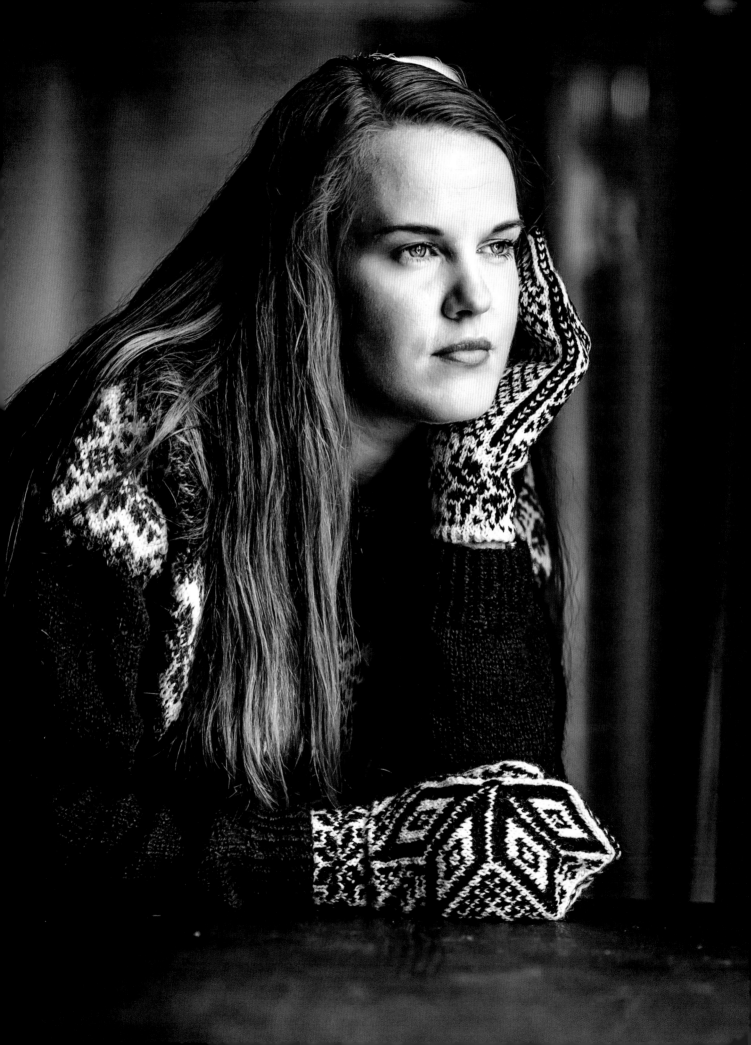

WOMEN'S MITTENS

‖‖‖

SIZE
Women's

FINISHED MEASUREMENTS
Circumference: approx. 9 in / 23 cm
Total Length: approx. 9 in / 23 cm

MATERIALS
Yarn:
CYCA #2 (sport, baby) Lofoten Wool Snykvit 2-ply
(100% pure Norwegian wool, 344 yd/315 m / 100 g)
CYCA #2 (sport, baby) Lofoten Wool Skarv 2-ply (100%
pure Norwegian wool, 344 yd/315 m / 100 g)

Alternate Yarn Suggestion:
CYCA #1 (fingering) Rauma 2-ply Gammelserie (100%
Norwegian wool, 175 yd/160 m / 50 g)

Yarn Colors and Amounts:
Snykvit (white): 100 g
Skarv (black): 100 g

Needles:
U. S. sizes 0 and 1.5 / 2 and 2.5 mm: sets of 5 dpn.

GAUGE
28 sts in pattern on larger needles = 4 in / 10 cm.
Adjust needle size to obtain correct gauge if necessary.

CUFF
With White and smaller dpn, CO 44 sts. Divide sts onto dpn and join. Work 4 rnds, k1 tbl, p1 ribbing. Change to larger dpn and knit 1 rnd, increasing 2 sts evenly spaced around = 46 sts. Work following Chart **A** for cuff = pattern section outlined in red.

MITTEN HAND
Continue following Chart **A**. Knit 1 rnd increasing 11 (sts evenly spaced around = 57 sts. Now work hand on Chart **A**, increasing for thumb gusset as shown on the chart. Increase with RLI for right-leaning increases and LLI for left-leaning.

At the red line above gusset on the chart, knit sts with smooth, contrast-color scrap yarn, which you will later remove. Slide the st back to left needle and knit in pattern. Alternatively, you can place the thumb sts on a holder and CO the same number of sts over the gap. Continue to top shaping. Decrease with k2tog for right-leaning decreases and with ssk or sl 1, k1, psso for left-leaning. When 10 sts rem, join sides with Kitchener st for a smooth finish or cut yarn and draw through rem sts; tighten.

THUMB
Worked on larger dpn. Insert a dpn through sts below scrap yarn and another dpn through sts above scrap yarn. Carefully remove scrap yarn. Or, knit live held sts and pick up and knit same number of sts along cast-on row of thumbhole. To avoid holes, pick up and knit 1 extra st at each corner = 28 sts for thumb.

Work following Chart **B**. Shape and finish top as for top of mitten.

Weave in all ends neatly on WS. Make left-hand mitten the same way, mirror-imaging the charts so the pair will show a large eight-petal rose when held together. Don't forget to place left thumb on left side of palm.

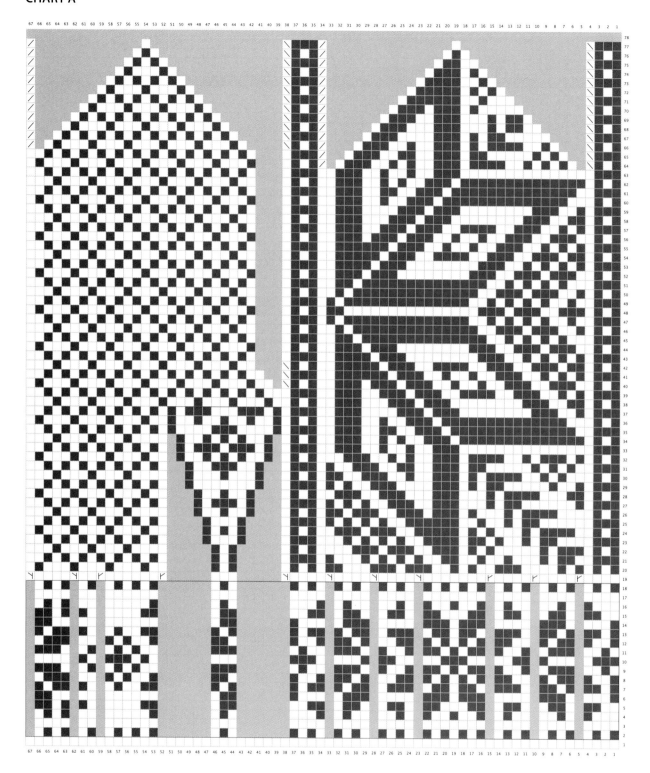

CHART B

☐	Snykvit (white)
■	Skarv (black)
＼	Ssk or sl 1, k1, psso
／	K2tog
☐	scrap yarn
Ⲑ	RLI
Ⳑ	LLI
▨	No stitch

SUNNFJORD MITTENS

One of my foremost sources of inspiration has been woven åkle *tapestry patterns; these tapestries have much in common with knitting. For the most part, their overall patterns are geometric, and I have carried this over to my mitten design. Sunnfjord is the region I come from. Many* åkle *tapestries with patterns similar to those on these mittens are on display at the Sunnfjord Museum, and that's how these mittens got their name.*

MEN'S MITTENS

SKILL LEVEL
Experienced

SIZE
Men's

FINISHED MEASUREMENTS
Circumference: approx. 10¼ in / 26 cm
Total Length: approx. 9¾ in / 25 cm

MATERIALS
Yarn:
CYCA #1 (fingering) Rauma 2-ply Gammelserie (100% Norwegian wool, 175 yd/160 m / 50 g)

Yarn Colors and Amounts:
White GL400: 50 g
Rust GL4904: 50 g

Needles:
U. S. sizes 0 and 1.5 / 2 and 2.5 mm: sets of 5 dpn.
NOTE: If you knit stranded colorwork more firmly than single-color knitting, you should go up a needle size.

GAUGE
28 sts in pattern on larger needles = 4 in / 10 cm.
Adjust needle size to obtain correct gauge if necessary.

CUFF
With White and smaller dpn, CO 54 sts. Divide sts onto dpn and join. Work 4 rnds, k1, p1 ribbing. Change to larger dpn and knit 1 rnd, increasing 6 sts evenly spaced around = 60 sts. Work following Chart **A** for cuff.

MITTEN HAND
After completing Chart **A**, knit 1 rnd increasing 5 sts evenly spaced around = 65 sts. Now work hand on Chart **B**, increasing for thumb gusset as shown on the chart. Increase with RLI for right-leaning increases and LLI for left-leaning.

At the red line above gusset on the chart, knit those sts with smooth, contrast-color scrap yarn, which you will later remove. Slide the sts back to left needle and knit in pattern. Alternatively, you can place the thumb sts on a holder and CO the same number of sts over the gap.

Continue, decreasing at the side of the thumb with k2tog where indicated on chart. To shape top, decrease with k2tog for right-leaning decreases and with ssk or sl 1, k1, psso for left-leaning. When 10 sts rem cut yarn and draw through rem sts; tighten.

CHART A

CHART C

THUMB

Worked on larger dpn. Insert a dpn through sts below scrap yarn and another dpn through sts above scrap yarn. Carefully remove scrap yarn. Or, knit live held sts and pick up and knit same number of sts along cast-on row of thumbhole. To avoid holes, pick up and knit 1 extra st at each corner = 32 sts for thumb.

Work following Chart **C**. Shape and finish top as for top of mitten.

Weave in all ends neatly on WS. Make left-hand mitten the same way, placing thumb gusset on left side of palm.

CHART B

	White GL400		LLI
	Rust GL4904		No stitch
	K2tog		Scrap yarn
	Ssk or sl 1, k1, psso		
	RLI		

WOMEN'S MITTENS

|||||||||||||||||||||||||||||||||||||||||||||||||||||||||||||||||||||||

SKILL LEVEL
Experienced

SIZE
Women's

FINISHED MEASUREMENTS
Circumference: approx. 9 in / 23 cm
Total Length: approx. 9¾ in / 25 cm

MATERIALS
Yarn:
CYCA #1 (fingering) Rauma 2-ply Gammelserie (100%
Norwegian wool, 175 yd/160 m / 50 g)

Yarn Colors and Amounts:
White GL400: 50 g
Rust GL4904: 50 g

Needles:
U. S. size 0 / 2 mm: sets of 5 dpn.
NOTE: If you knit stranded colorwork more firmly than
single-color knitting, you should go up a needle size.

GAUGE
28 sts in pattern on larger needles = 4 in / 10 cm
Adjust needle size to obtain correct gauge if necessary.

CUFF

Can be worked in either a narrow or (wide) version. With Rust, CO 56 (64) sts. Divide sts onto dpn and join. Purl 1 rnd.
Lace Cuff:
Rnd 1: Change to White and work *p1, k2tog, k4 (5), yo, k1, yo, k4 (5), k2tog*; rep * to * around.
Rnd 2: Work knit over knit and purl over purl.
Rnd 3: Work as for Rnd 1.
Rnd 4: Work as for Rnd 2.
Rnd 5: Change to Rust and work as for Rnd 1.
Rnd 6: Purl around.
Rep Rnds 1-6 until you've worked a total of 26 rnds. End with knit 1 rnd with White.

MITTEN HAND

After completing lace cuff. Knit 1 rnd, and, *on narrow cuff only*, increase 8 sts evenly spaced around = 64 sts. Now work hand following Chart **A**, increasing for thumb gusset as shown on chart. Increase with RLI for right-leaning increases and LLI for left-leaning. At the red line above gusset on the chart, knit sts with smooth, contrast-color scrap yarn, which you will later remove. Slide the sts back to left needle and knit in pattern. Alternatively, you can place the thumb sts on a holder and CO the same number of sts over the gap.

Continue, decreasing at the side of the thumb with k2tog where indicated on chart. To shape top, decrease with k2tog for right-leaning decreases and with ssk or sl 1, k1, psso for left-leaning. When 10 sts rem, cut yarn and draw through rem sts; tighten.

CHART A

White GL400   ⋎ RLI

■ Rust GL4904   ⋏ LLI

╱ K2tog   Scrap yarn

╲ Ssk or sl 1, k1, psso

   No stitch

96

THUMB

Worked on larger dpn. Insert a dpn through sts below scrap yarn and another dpn through sts above scrap yarn. Carefully remove scrap yarn. Or, knit live held sts and pick up and knit same number of sts along cast-on row of thumbhole. To avoid holes, pick up and knit 1 extra st at each corner = 28 sts for thumb.

Work following Chart **B**. Shape and finish top as for top of mitten.

Weave in all ends neatly on WS. Make left-hand mitten the same way, placing thumb gusset on left side of palm.

CHART B

SNOWSTORM HAT

The snowstorm hat gets its name from the snowflake-like lice in the pattern. This is a detailed, fun, and challenging design to knit. The pattern and folded brim make the hat rather long. If you want a less baggy version, you can begin on Row 25 of the pattern.

||||||||||||||||||||||||||||||||||||||||||||||||||||||||||||||||||

SKILL LEVEL
Experienced

SIZE
One size fits all

FINISHED MEASUREMENTS
Circumference: approx. 21¾ in / 55 cm
Total Length: approx. 9 (11¾) in / 23 (30) cm

MATERIALS
Yarn:
CYCA #1 (fingering) Pickles Pure Wool (100% wool, 414 yd/379 m / 100 g)

Yarn Colors and Amounts:
Avalanche 104: 100 g
Winter Night: 100 g

Needles:
U. S. sizes 1.5 and 4 / 2.5 and 3.5 mm: short circulars and sets of 5 dpn.

GAUGE
26 sts in pattern on larger needles = 4 in / 10 cm.
Adjust needle size to obtain correct gauge if necessary.

CASTING ON

With smaller circular or dpn and Winter Night, CO 118 sts. Join, being careful not to twist cast-on row; pm for beginning of rnd. Work 20 rnds in k1, p1 ribbing. Work 3 rnds with knit over purl and purl over knit for foldline.

HAT

Knit 1 rnd, increasing 10 sts evenly spaced around = 128 sts. Change to larger size needle (change to dpn when sts no longer fit around circular). Work following chart, decreasing to shape crown as shown.

Double Decrease: Sl 1, k2tog in pattern color, psso.

After completing charted rows, cut yarn and draw end through rem sts; tighten.

Weave in all ends neatly on WS.

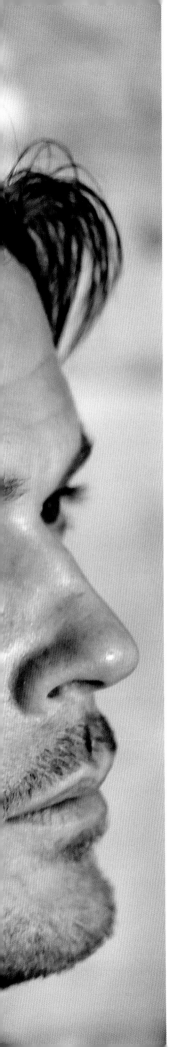

☐ Avalanche 104

■ Winter Night

∧ Double decrease—
see pattern instructions

☐ Short version

▨ No stitch

CABLE HAT

This hat design was inspired by cable-knitted folk costume stockings. The hat fits most adult heads and will be attractive in almost any color. If you don't like the color I used in the pattern, feel free to choose your own—but make it a solid color, because heathers have a tendency to hide the structure of cable knitting.

|||||||||||||||||||||||||||||||||||||||||||||||||||||||||||||||||

SKILL LEVEL
Experienced

SIZE
One size fits all

FINISHED MEASUREMENTS
Circumference: approx. 21¾-23¾ in / 55-60 cm depending on gauge
Total Length: approx. 9¾ in / 25 cm

MATERIALS
Yarn:
CYCA #2 (sport, baby) Rauma Finull PT2 (100% Norwegian wool, 191 yd/175 m / 50 g)

Yarn Color and Amount:
Dark Mustard 4065: 100 g

Needles:
U. S. sizes 0 and 2.5 / 2 and 3 mm: set of 5 dpn; cable needle.

GAUGE
26 sts in cable pattern on larger needles = 4 in / 10 cm.
Adjust needle size to obtain correct gauge if necessary.

CASTING ON AND BRIM
With smaller dpn, CO 128 sts. Join, being careful not to twist cast-on row; pm for beginning of rnd. Work 20 rnds in k2, p2 ribbing. Work 2 rnds with knit over purl and purl over knit for foldline.

HAT
Change to larger dpn and knit 1 rnd, increasing 8 sts evenly spaced around = 136 sts. The hat can be made as long or short as you like by repeating or omitting repeats in the section outlined in red on the chart. The hat shown in the photos was worked with two complete repeats in length before the crown shaping.

Decrease for crown as shown on the chart. K2tog for right-leaning decreases and ssk or sl 1, k1, psso for left-leaning decreases. After completing charted rows, cut yarn and draw end through rem sts; tighten.

Weave in all ends neatly on WS. Gently steam press hat under a damp pressing cloth—make sure you don't flatten the cables.

Knit

Place 2 sts on cable needle and hold in back of work; k2 from left needle and then k2 from cable needle.

• Purl

Place 2 sts on cable needle and hold in front of work; k2 from left needle and then k2 from cable needle.

Repeat to desired length

/ K2tog—right-leaning decrease

\ Ssk or sl 1, k1, psso—left-leaning decrease

No stitch

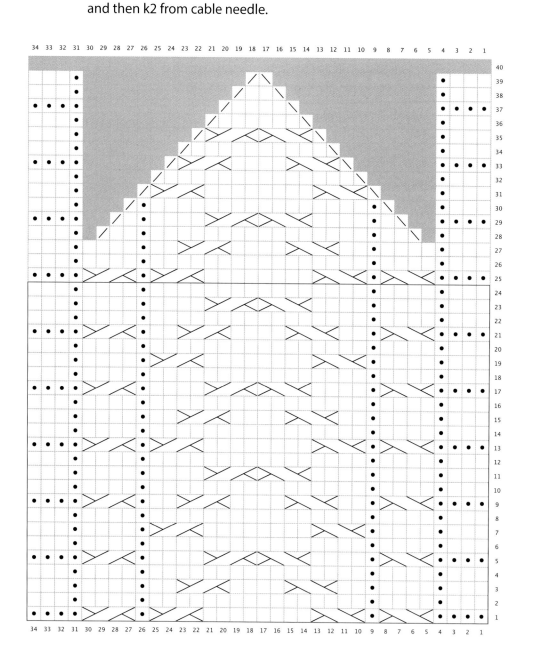

FOREST STAR HAT

This Forest Star hat was inspired by an old pair of socks displayed in a digital museum. The pattern is distinguished by large diamonds filled with eight-point stars edged by the "Pine" or spruce pattern, which is a classic way of filling in the corners of star or rose motifs.

||||||||||||||||||||||||||||||||||||||||||||||||||||||||||||||||||||||||||||

SKILL LEVEL
Experienced

SIZE
One size fits all

FINISHED MEASUREMENTS
Circumference: approx. 21¾ in / 55 cm
Total Length: approx. 10¾ in / 27 cm

MATERIALS
Yarn:
CYCA #1 (fingering) Trollkar Supermjuk (Supersoft)
(100% pure new wool, 383 yd/350 m / 100 g)

Yarn Colors and Amounts:
Natural White 201: 100 g
Pine Needles 360: 100 g

Needles:
U. S. sizes 1.5 and 4 / 2.5 and 3.5 mm: short circulars
and sets of 5 dpn.

GAUGE
26 sts in pattern on larger needles = 4 in / 10 cm.
Adjust needle size to obtain correct gauge if necessary.

HAT

With smaller circular or dpn and Pine Needles, CO 132 sts. Join, being careful not to twist cast-on row; pm for beginning of rnd. Work 20 rnds in k1, p1 ribbing. Change to larger size needle (change to dpn when sts no longer fit around circular).

Knit 1 rnd, increasing 12 sts evenly spaced around = 144 sts. Work following chart, beginning at lower right corner and working to the first decrease rnd. Decrease to shape crown as shown.

Double Decrease: Sl 1, k2tog in pattern color, psso.

After completing charted rows, 6 sts rem. Cut yarn and draw end through rem sts; tighten. Weave in all ends neatly on WS.

CHART

Natural White 201

Pine Needles 360

No stitch

∧ Double decrease—
see pattern instructions

109

TOP STAR HAT

The eight-petal rose on this hat reminded me of an eight-point star—the kind of star you might see at the top of a Christmas tree. The geometric pattern lends itself well to perfect divisions for decreasing, a fine detail on a hat crown.

||||||||||||||||||||||||||||||||||||||||||||||||||||||||

SKILL LEVEL
Experienced

SIZE
One size fits all

FINISHED MEASUREMENTS
Circumference: approx. 21¾ in / 55 cm
Total Length: approx. 8¾ (10¾) in / 22 (27) cm

MATERIALS
Yarn:
CYCA #1 (fingering) Trollkar Supermjuk (Supersoft)
(100% pure new wool, 383 yd/350 m / 100 g)

Yarn Colors and Amounts:
Golden Brown 292: 100 g
Natural White 201: 100 g

Needles:
U. S. sizes 1.5 and 4 / 2.5 and 3.5 mm: short circulars
and sets of 5 dpn.

GAUGE
26 sts in pattern on larger needles = 4 in / 10 cm.
Adjust needle size to obtain correct gauge if necessary.

HAT

With smaller circular or dpn and Golden Brown, CO 132 sts. Join, being careful not to twist cast-on row; pm for beginning of rnd. Work 20 rnds in k1, p1 ribbing. Change to larger needle (change to dpn when sts no longer fit around circular).

Knit 1 rnd, increasing 12 sts evenly spaced around = 144 sts. Work following chart, beginning at lower right corner. If you want a shorter hat, begin on the row marked in red on the chart. Continue to the first decrease rnd. Decrease to shape crown as shown.

Double Decrease: Sl 1, k2tog in color indicated on chart, psso.

After completing charted rows, cut yarn and draw end through rem sts; tighten. Weave in all ends neatly on WS.

CHART

Natural White 201

Golden Brown 292

Short version

∧ Double decrease—
see pattern instructions

No stitch

FLOWERPOT COVER

Upcycling is a major trend in Norway these days; it involves taking something you might usually throw away and making it into something new instead. If you eat a lot of yogurt, you can upcycle the cups into little flowerpots—and then knit some covers for them.

SKILL LEVEL
Experienced

SIZE
Will fit a large yogurt cup

MATERIALS
Yarn:
CYCA #1 (fingering) Sandnes Garn Sisu (80% wool, 20% nylon, approx. 191 yd/175 m / 50 g)

Yarn Colors and Amounts:
White 1001: 50 g
Charcoal Heather 1088: 50 g

Needles:
U. S. size 0 / 2 mm: set of 5 dpn.

Crochet Hook:
U. S. size A / 2 mm

GAUGE
30 sts in pattern = 4 in / 10 cm.
Adjust needle size to obtain correct gauge if necessary.

COVER

With dpn and White, CO 88 sts. Divide sts onto dpn and join. Knit 1 rnd. Work in pattern following chart until cover is 4¾ in / 12 cm long or desired height.

Crochet the top of the cover: work 1 sc in each knitted st around. Work 4 more rnds sc. Join last st with a sl st, cut yarn and fasten off.

BASE

Crochet the base: ch 5, and join last ch to first with 1 sl st.

Rnd 1: Work 8 sc around ring and join with 1 sl st.
Rnd 2: Work 2 sc in each sc of rnd below = 16 sc.
Rnd 3: Beginning in sc nearest hook, *work 1 sc, work 2 sc in next sc*; rep * to * around = 24 sc.
Rnd 4: *Work 1 sc in each of next two sc, 2 sc in next sc*; rep * to * around = 32 sc.
Rnd 5: *Work 1 sc in each of next three sc, 2 sc in next sc*; rep * to * around = 40 sc.

Continue increasing on every rnd with 1 more sc between increases on each rnd until base is large enough to cover bottom of cup. Finish by cutting yarn and fastening off. Sew base to cover around cast-on edge.

Weave in all ends neatly on WS.

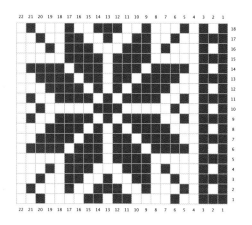

☐ White 1001
■ Charcoal Heather 1088

114

BOTTLE COZY

There are so many handy water bottles to buy, and it might be fun to knit a lovely cover for yours. Instead of using the suggested yarn, you can dive into your stash, as this pattern doesn't require much yarn.

||||||||||||||||||||||||||||||||||||||||||||||||||||||||||||||||

SKILL LEVEL
Experienced

SIZE
Cozy will fit over a bottle 8¼ in / 21 cm around and 8¾ in / 22 cm high

MATERIALS
Yarn:
CYCA #2 (sport, baby) Rauma Finull PT2 (100% Norwegian wool, 191 yd/175 m / 50 g)
OR use leftover yarn from your stash—you don't need much

Yarn Colors and Amounts:
Natural White 401: 50 g
Asphalt 4387: 50 g
Burnt Orange 434: 50 g
A little length of yarn for the hanging loop

Needles:
U. S. size 2.5 / 3 mm: set of 5 dpn.

Crochet Hook:
U. S. size D-3 / 3 mm

GAUGE
26 sts in pattern = 4 in / 10 cm.
Adjust needle size to obtain correct gauge if necessary.

COVER

With dpn and White, CO 56 sts. Divide sts onto dpn and join. Knit 1 rnd. Work in pattern following chart until cover is 8 in / 20 cm long or desired height. Knit 1 rnd White.

HANGING LOOP

With Orange (or your choice of color) and crochet hook, make a chain 8 in / 20 cm long and join into a ring with 1 sl st into 1st ch = hanging loop. Now you will use the hook to bind off the sts on the knitting needles. Insert hook through 2 loops on first dpn, yarnover hook and through the 2 loops. Yarn over hook and through the 2 loops you now have on hook. Rep this process until you've bound off all the sts around. To finish, work sc all around the hanging loop, joining with 1 sl st in first st of bind-off.

BASE

Crochet the base: work 4 ch, and join last ch to first with 1 sl st.
Rnd 1: Ch 1, work 7 sc around ring and join with 1 sl st.
Rnd 2: Ch 1, work *1 sc in next sc, 2 sc in next sc*; rep * to * around = 10 sc.
Rnd 3: *Work 1 sc in each of next two sc, 2 sc in next sc*; rep * to * around = 13 sc.
Rnd 4: *Work 1 sc in each of next three sc, 2 sc in next sc*; rep * to * around = 16 sc.

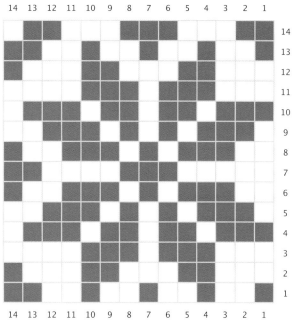

| 14 | 13 | 12 | 11 | 10 | 9 | 8 | 7 | 6 | 5 | 4 | 3 | 2 | 1 | |

Continue increasing on every rnd with 1 more sc between increases on each rnd until base is large enough. Finish by cutting yarn and fastening off. Weave in all ends neatly on WS. Sew base to cover around cast-on edge.

☐ Natural White 401

■ Asphalt 4387

POTHOLDERS

Knitted and crocheted potholders are fun projects with quick results. These potholders are a good beginner project if you aren't experienced with two-color stranded knitting. Made with heavy cotton yarn and two layers, it'll be almost impossible to burn yourself when using them.

‖‖‖

SKILL LEVEL
Experienced

FINISHED MEASUREMENTS
Width: approx. 9 in / 23 cm

MATERIALS
Yarn:
CYCA #5 (bulky) Sandnes Garn Mandarin Grande
(100% cotton, 61 yd/56 m / 50 g)

Yarn Colors and Amounts:
White 1001: 100 g
Black 1099: 100 g
Raisin 4362: 50 g

Needles:
U. S. size 8 / 5 mm: set of 5 dpn or short circular.
NOTE: If you knit stranded colorwork more firmly than single-color knitting, you should go up a needle size.

Crochet Hook:
U. S. size 7 / 4.5 mm

GAUGE
15 sts in stockinette = 4 in / 10 cm.
Adjust needle size to obtain correct gauge if necessary.

CASTING ON

The potholder is worked in the round. With White, CO 68 sts. Join and pm for beginning of rnd. Work 1 rnd as follows: k33, p1, k33, p1. The purl sts mark each side between the back and front and will be used later for crocheting on the edging.

POTHOLDER

Work in pattern following the chart, maintaining purl side sts until you complete charted rows. End with 1 rnd: k33, p1, k33, p1. BO. Weave in all ends neatly on WS.

JOINING WITH CROCHET

With Raisin or your choice of color, crochet to join the pieces and make a hanging loop. Begin at top right corner of potholder with the hanging loop: ch 10. Join into a ring with sl st into 1st ch. Join the loops of bind-off row on each side with 1 sc in each pair of sts. Work 3 sc in corner and then work 1 sc in each purl st along edge, 3 sc in corner and then join cast-on row with sc as for bind-off row. Work 3 sc in corner and 1 sc in each purl st along edge. Finish with 10 sc around loop at beginning of rnd. Work another rnd of sc all around edge, with 3 sc in each corner st. End at loop. Do not work more sc around loop. Cut yarn and fasten off.

FINISHING

Weave in rem ends to WS. Gently steam press potholder under a damp pressing cloth.

34 33 32 31 30 29 28 27 26 25 24 23 22 21 20 19 18 17 16 15 14 13 12 11 10 9 8 7 6 5 4 3 2 1

White 1001

• Purl

Black 1099

TRADITIONAL TIE

Knitted ties are a well-established phenomenon, although usually you'll see machine-knitted garter stitch versions. Here's one in authentic Selbu style. It might seem a little tricky at first, but once you've got the hang of it, it's easy to knit.

||||||||||||||||||||||||||||||||||||||||||||||||||||||||||||||||||

SKILL LEVEL
Experienced

FINISHED MEASUREMENTS
Width: approx. 1¾ in / 4.5 cm
Total Length: approx. 21¼ in / 54 cm or desired length

MATERIALS
Yarn:
CYCA #0 (lace) Brooklyn Tweed Vale (100% Rambouillet wool, 450 yd/411 m / 50 g)

Yarn Colors and Amounts:
Klimt 538: 100 g
Sashiko 566: 100 g

Notions:
Hook and eye set

Needles:
U. S. size 0 / 2 mm: set of 5 dpn.
NOTE: If you knit stranded colorwork more firmly than single-color knitting, you should go up a needle size.

Crochet Hook:
U. S. size A / 2 mm

GAUGE
54 sts in stockinette = 4 in / 10 cm.
Adjust needle size to obtain correct gauge if necessary.

CASTING ON

With Sashiko, CO 52 sts. Divide sts onto dpn and join. Knit 1 rnd.

TIE

Work following Chart **A** for front and Chart **B** for back. Work around in pattern as est until tie is 21¼ in / 54 cm long or desired length. Keep in mind that part of the tie will be hidden in the knot. BO.

KNOT

This tie has a faux knot. With Sashiko, CO 52 sts. Divide sts onto dpn and join. Work as for tie until 2 in / 5 cm long. BO. Sew each end of the knot together, leaving an opening of about ⅝ in / 1.5 cm at the top of both ends so you can draw the neckband through. The knot should resemble an actual knot at the top of a tie. Sew into place.

NECKBAND

Ch 8 with crochet hook. Work back and forth in sc over 8 sts until band is 12¾ in / 32 cm long. On the last row, make a chain loop: work 1 sc, ch 6, 1 sc in last sc of row. Turn and work a row of sc across loop. Cut yarn and pull end through last loop; fasten off. Draw band through hole in knot and sew into place. Sew on a hook and eye set small enough that it can be hooked through the crocheted band and the tie can be adjusted around your neck.

FINISHING

Weave in all ends neatly on WS. Gently steam press tie under a damp pressing cloth.

CHART A

☐ Klimt 538

■ Sashiko 566

CHART B

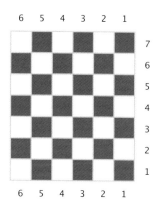

BOWTIE

Bowties are a fun accessory that can set the tone both for your outfit and the day. This project will appeal to both grandad and the hipster on the street.

‖‖‖

SKILL LEVEL
Experienced

FINISHED MEASUREMENTS
Width: approx. 4¼ in / 11 cm

MATERIALS
Yarn:
CYCA #0 (lace) Brooklyn Tweed Vale (100% Rambouillet wool, 450 yd/411 m / 50 g)

Yarn Colors and Amounts:
Klimt 538: 100 g
Sashiko 566: 100 g

Notions:
Hook and eye set

Needles:
U. S. size 0 / 2 mm: set of 5 dpn.
NOTE: If you knit stranded colorwork more firmly than single-color knitting, you should go up a needle size.

Crochet Hook:
U. S. size A / 2 mm

GAUGE
52 sts in stockinette = 4 in / 10 cm.
Adjust needle size to obtain correct gauge if necessary.

CASTING ON
With Sashiko, CO 52 sts. Divide sts onto dpn and join. Knit 1 rnd.

BOW
Work following Chart A for 2 repeats in length. End with Row 1 of chart and then BO.

KNOT
This tie has a faux knot. With Sashiko, CO 24 sts. Divide sts onto dpn and join. Knit 1 rnd. Work following Chart **B** until piece measures approx. 3¼ in / 8 cm. Knit 1 rnd with Sashiko and then BO. Fold the knot around the center of the bow and sew it neatly into place for a proper bowtie.

NECKBAND
With Sashiko and crochet hook, ch 8. Work back and forth in sc over 8 sts until band is 12¾ in / 32 cm long. On the last row, make a chain loop: work 1 sc, ch 6, 1 sc in last sc of row. Turn and work a row of sc across loop. Cut yarn and pull end through last loop; fasten off.

Sew the band neatly to the back of the bowtie. Sew on a hook and eye set small enough that it can be hooked through the crocheted band and the tie can be adjusted around your neck.

FINISHING
Weave in all ends neatly on WS. Gently steam press bowtie under a damp pressing cloth.

CHART A

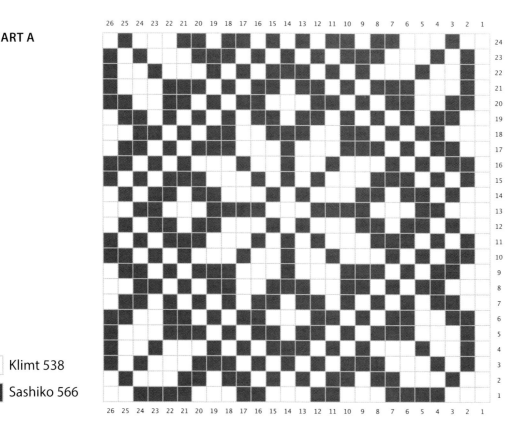

□ Klimt 538
■ Sashiko 566

CHART B

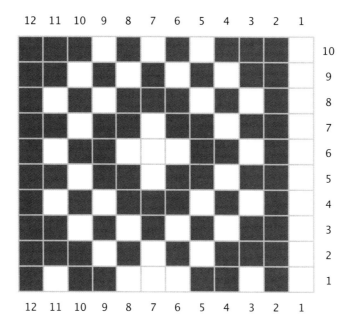

WOMEN'S BELT

A traditional tie can also be used as a simple dress belt by omitting the knot and knitting the same pattern on front and back. Tying a belt with a single knot is an easy way to show off the waist of a dress. This belt has much in common with motifs found on embroidered and woven bands and belts worn with folk costumes.

SKILL LEVEL
Experienced

FINISHED MEASUREMENTS
Width: approx. 2 in / 5 cm
Total Length: approx. 47¼ in / 120 cm

MATERIALS
Yarn:
CYCA #0 (lace) Brooklyn Tweed Vale (100% Rambouillet wool, 450 yd/411 m / 50 g)

Yarn Colors and Amounts:
Barberry 523: 100 g
Nocturne 568: 100 g

Needles:
U. S. size 0 / 2 mm: set of 5 dpn.
NOTE: If you knit stranded colorwork more firmly than single-color knitting, you should go up a needle size.

GAUGE
52 sts in stockinette = 4 in / 10 cm.
Adjust needle size to obtain correct gauge if necessary.

☐ Barberry 523
■ Nocturne 568

BELT
With Barberry, CO 52 sts. Divide sts onto dpn and join. Knit 1 rnd. Work following Chart **A** for both front and back of belt. When piece measures 47¼ in / 120 cm or desired length, BO.

FINISHING
Sew each end of belt so it lies flat. Weave in all ends neatly on WS. Gently steam press belt under a damp pressing cloth.

CHART A

SMALL COVERS

Small covers are a good beginner project for anyone not experienced with two-color stranded knitting. One simple chart works for several items. Here, the same pattern is used for covers for a soda can and a little vase.

IIIIIIIIIIIIIIIIIIIIIIIIIIIIIIIIIIIIIIIIIIIIIIIIIIIIIIIIIIIIIIIIIIIIIIIIII

SKILL LEVEL
Experienced

SIZES
Fits a glass bottle or aluminum can about 6¼ (8¼) in / 16 (21) cm in circumference

MATERIALS
Yarn:
CYCA #1 (fingering) Sandnes Garn Sisu (80% wool, 20% nylon, approx. 191 yd/175 m / 50 g)

Yarn Colors and Amounts:
White 1001: 50 (50) g
Charcoal Heather 1088: 50 (50) g

Needles:
U. S. size 0 / 2 mm: set of 5 dpn.
NOTE: If you knit stranded colorwork more firmly than single-color knitting, you should go up a needle size.

Crochet Hook:
U. S. size A / 2 mm

GAUGE
30 sts in stockinette = 4 in / 10 cm.
Adjust needle size to obtain correct gauge if necessary.

COVER
With White, CO 40 (64) sts. Divide sts onto dpn. Join and knit 1 rnd.

Now work around following charted pattern. Work 2 rep in length or to desired length.

Bind off with crochet hook: slip 1st st onto hook. *Insert hook through the next 2 sts on needle, yarn over hook, and draw yarn through 2 loops; 2 loops rem on hook. Yarn over hook and through 2 loops*. Rep * to * until all the sts have been bound off.

BASE
Crochet the base: Ch 5 and join last ch to first with 1 sl st.
Rnd 1: Work 8 sc around ring and join with 1 sl st.
Rnd 2: Work 2 sc in each sc of rnd below = 16 sc.
Rnd 3: Beginning in sc nearest hook, *work 1 sc, work 2 sc in next sc*; rep * to * around = 24 sc.
Rnd 4: *Work 1 sc in each of next two sc, 2 sc in next sc*; rep * to * around = 32 sc.
Rnd 5: *Work 1 sc in each of next three sc, 2 sc in next sc*; rep * to * around = 40 sc.
Continue increasing on every rnd with 1 more sc between increases on each rnd until base is large enough to cover bottom of object. Finish by cutting yarn and fastening off.

FINISHING
Weave in all ends neatly on WS.
Sew base to cover around cast-on edge.
Gently steam press cover under damp pressing cloth.
Pull cover onto lamp foot/bottle/vase.

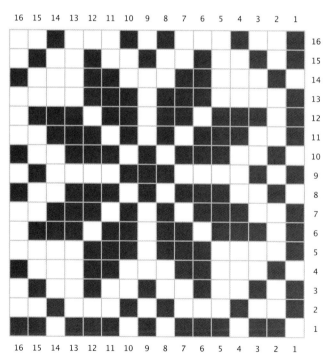

White 1001

Charcoal Heather 1088

YARN RESOURCES

BROOKLYN TWEED
www.brooklyntweed.com

HILLESVÅG ULLVAREFABRIKK
www.ull.no; post@ull.no

LOFOTEN WOOL
www.lofoten-wool.no; lofoten-wool@hotmail.com

PICKLES
www.pickles.no

RAUMA ULLVAREFABRIKK
Finull PT2 and Gammelserie available from
www.thewoollythistle.com; www.theyarnguys.com

SANDNES ULLVAREFABRIKK
See www.sandnes-garn.com for a list of distributors
In the U. S., www.theloopyewe.com sells Peer Gynt
and Smart

TROLLKAR
www.trollkar.no; kontakt@trollkar.no

Some yarns may be difficult to find. A variety of additional and substitute yarns are available from:

WEBS – AMERICA'S YARN STORE
75 Service Center Road
Northampton, MA 01060
800-367-9327
yarn.com

LOVEKNITTING.COM
loveknitting.com/us

If you are unable to obtain any of the yarn used in this book, it can be replaced with a yarn of a similar weight and composition. Please note, however, the finished projects may vary slightly from those shown, depending on the yarn used. Try www.yarnsub.com for suggestions.

For more information on selecting or substituting yarn, contact your local yarn shop or an online store; they are familiar with all types of yarns and would be happy to help you. Additionally, the online knitting community at Ravelry.com has forums where you can post questions about specific yarns. Yarns come and go so quickly these days and there are so many beautiful yarns available.